The
FRIENDSHIP
of NATURE

AMERICAN LAND CLASSICS

Charles E. Little, *Series Editor*

George F. Thompson, *Series Director*

American Land Classics makes available to a new generation of readers enduring works on geography, landscape, nature, and place.

Published in cooperation with the Center for American Places, Santa Fe, New Mexico, and Harrisonburg, Virginia

The
FRIENDSHIP
of NATURE

A New England Chronicle
of Birds and Flowers

by

MABEL OSGOOD WRIGHT

with photographs by the author

edited by

DANIEL J. PHILIPPON

The Johns Hopkins University Press
Baltimore and London

This book was brought to publication with the generous assistance
of the Connecticut Audubon Society, in celebration of its
centennial, in 1998.

The Friendship of Nature: A New England Chronicle of Birds and Flowers
was originally published in 1894 in a hardcover edition by
Macmillan and Company, New York and London.

The Johns Hopkins University Press
2715 North Charles Street
Baltimore, Maryland 21218-4363
www.press.jhu.edu

Library of Congress Cataloging-in-Publication Data
will be found at the end of this book.
A catalog record for this book is available from the British Library.

ISBN 0-8018-6234-5
ISBN 0-8018-6223-X (pbk.)

Contents

Illustrations

A Note on the Text

The text of *The Friendship of Nature* has been reset from the original hardcover edition published by Macmillan and Company in 1894. British spellings have been preserved, but obvious spelling errors have been silently corrected. Wright's hyphenations also have been preserved. End-line hyphenations were rendered in modern form only when Wright's usage was unclear. Chapter epigraphs have been reformatted for consistency.

All photographs, with the exception of the frontispiece, were taken and titled by Mabel Osgood Wright and are reproduced courtesy of the Fairfield Historical Society.

The notes at the end of the volume provide sources and additional information for material cited in the introduction. They also identify quotations, define unfamiliar or obscure words and phrases, and further clarify Wright's text. Except in a few instances, no attempt has been made to provide or define botanical and scientific terms. Common and scientific names of species are referenced in the index.

On 18 March 1894, Mabel Osgood Wright dedicated *The Friendship of Nature* to the memory of her father, Samuel Osgood:

> If love a debt can pay
> As well as gold,
> Think me not bold
> When I seek to return,
> By loving, all I learn
> of nature every day.

Acknowledgments

First and foremost among the many individuals who have aided me in the rediscovery of Mabel Osgood Wright has been Christopher Nevins, the indefatigable director of the Connecticut Audubon Society's Birdcraft Museum and Sanctuary, whose enthusiasm, wide-ranging knowledge, and unwavering support have made this project a pleasure to pursue. Alison Olivieri, Robert Braun, Suzanna Nyberg, Lauren Brown, Sherman Kent, and other members of the Connecticut Audubon family have also aided me in my research; they have my deep gratitude. Special thanks to Henrietta and Robert Lachman for opening their home to me and educating me in the fine points of early American pottery. For friendly and helpful conversations about Wright and her legacy, I would also like to acknowledge Becky Abbott, Virginia Lopez Begg, and Betsy Mendelsohn.

For their invaluable research assistance, I am indebted to Barbara Austen of the Fairfield Historical Society, Peggy Wargo and Tom Geoffino of the Fairfield Public Library, Mary Witkowski in the Historical Collections of the Bridgeport Public Library, Mary LeCroy in the Ornithology Department of the American Museum of Natural History, John Stinson in the Rare Books and Manuscripts Division of the New York Public Library, and the reference and interlibrary loan staffs of the University of Virginia Library.

For institutional support, I am grateful to the Department of English at the University of Virginia and the Department of Rhetoric at the University of Minnesota, Twin Cities.

For their close reading of the introduction, I would like to thank Michael P. Branch, Alan B. Howard, George F. Thompson, and Tom Roche, each of whom aided this project in unique ways. I thank Mike for his continued inspiration, Alan for his unending patience, George for his wise counsel and editorial acumen, and Tom for his careful copyediting. All four deserve more thanks than I can offer here.

To my parents, Benoit and Trudy Philippon, whose proximity to

Fairfield made my visits home that much shorter, I offer my gratitude, and to the many other friends and colleagues who have provided support and guidance, I offer my heartfelt thanks. All errors are of course my own.

The
FRIENDSHIP
of NATURE

Introduction

W HEN the history of these times is written there will surely be a place in it for Mabel Osgood Wright," one Connecticut editorialist noted confidently following Wright's death in 1934. "Fairfield . . . will have to share Mrs. Wright with the rest of the world when time has demonstrated the profound influence which she exercised through her writings and personal efforts, in the field of nature study and bird protection." Sixty-five years later, Wright's time has finally come.

Author of twenty-five works of fiction and nonfiction, founder of the Connecticut Audubon Society, for twelve years associate editor of *Bird-Lore* magazine (now *Audubon*), an accomplished landscape photographer, and the organizing force behind one of the first privately owned bird sanctuaries in the United States, Mabel Osgood Wright is not only a neglected writer and illustrator but also a lost hero of the American conservation movement, one whose work became a model for local wildlife and habitat preservation efforts throughout the country. As another writer noted upon Wright's passing, "No other author of her time did more than Mrs. Wright to arouse and sustain interest in nature, and the great change in the public's attitude toward nature and wild things over a generation has been due in no small degree to her educative efforts." *The Friendship of Nature* (1894), Wright's first book and her most accomplished work of nature writing for adults, remains the finest literary monument to her achievements in nature appreciation, education, and conservation.

Along with another popular nature writer's first book—John Muir's *The Mountains of California*, published the same year—*The Friendship of Nature* helped to inaugurate the "back-to-nature" movement that swept the nation during the first decades of the twentieth century. As Wright observed in 1903, however, "It is not a 'going back to Nature' as it is often called, for any backward movement is to be deplored; not a relapse to insensate savagery, but a stepping forward, with keen understanding eyes and outstretched hands, to meet Nature upon the higher plane of the desire of perfect mental and physical understanding." As its title suggests, *The Friendship of Nature* offers not "a relapse to insensate savagery" but a far gentler view of nature, one populated with neighborly birds and flowers and defined by the seasonal changes Wright observed around her Connecticut home. Moreover, her descriptions of nature are grounded in ornithology and botany, informed by classical mythology and the experience of women, and constructed upon the premise that human beings are intimately connected to the landscapes in which they live and work. Written at a time when nature was valued mainly for its grandeur and sublimity, *The Friendship of Nature* challenged its readers to appreciate the land on a local, personal, and familiar level—to turn their gaze from the awe-inspiring spectacles that were being given National Park status at the time and to rediscover the beauty and complexity of their own backyards.

More than one hundred years after its initial publication, *The Friendship of Nature* deserves renewed attention as a precursor of the current "back-to-nature" movement, whose curbside recycling programs, organic farmers' markets, and annual Earth Day celebrations fulfill Wright's definition of "a stepping forward." If Americans at the dawn of the twentieth century turned to nature as a refuge from urbanization and industrialization, today more and more people are recognizing that the idea of an independent "nature"—one unrelated to human activity—can no longer be supported, that nature is in fact an integral part of everyday life. At the same time, they are also recognizing that the physical reality of nature is being destroyed at an unprecedented rate, perhaps even precipitating what the naturalist E. O. Wilson calls "the sixth great extinction spasm" in evolutionary history. ("I am very glad," wrote Wright in 1902, "that I shall not be alive when the world's water is all utilized, the marshes drained, the weeds subdued, a universal insecticide invented, all waste-land reclaimed. What a horrible, lonely, selfish world it will be.") In the face of this seemingly relentless march of "progress," *The Friendship of Nature* and its author still have much to teach people about an appropriate relationship to nature, as both a physical reality and a cultural construct. Just as *The Friendship of Nature* remains an effective argument for cultivating humility and finding value in the local landscape, so does the life of Mabel Osgood Wright offer a model for conservationists who wish to sway public opinion about the need to preserve wild things and the environments they inhabit. Few lessons could be more important, or more necessary, today.

BIOGRAPHY

An Influential Father

One cannot fully appreciate the life of Mabel Osgood Wright without first knowing something about her father, Unitarian minister Samuel Osgood (1812–80), for it was from him that Wright learned to appreciate what became the two most important things in her life: books and nature. He also introduced her to her future husband, provided her with a model of literary and cultural achievement, and built the home that sustained her during her most productive years of writing. Moreover, his Victorian beliefs about the proper role of women and the significance of country life offer landmarks from which we can gauge the progress of his daughter in successfully navigating her passage into the modern world.

A student of the Unitarian ministers Henry Ware and William Ellery Channing, whose work he encountered at the Harvard Divinity School, Osgood was a tireless writer and speaker, his enthusiasm for intellectual life tempered only by his love of gardening. He was an editor of the *Western Messenger* and the *Christian Inquirer*, both Unitarian journals; a contributor to the *North American Review*, *Putnam's*, *Harper's*, and other periodicals; and the author of six major volumes of essays, sermons, and speeches. A member of William Cullen Bryant's literary circle, Osgood counted among his friends some of the most prominent men of letters in the nineteenth century, including George Bancroft, Oliver Wendell Holmes, Edmund Clarence Stedman, Edwin Arnold, George William Curtis, Edwin Booth, Lawrence Barrett, William Wetmore Story, John Hay, and Joseph Choate.

After beginning his ministry in New Hampshire and Rhode Island during the 1830s and 1840s, and after marrying Ellen Haswell Murdoch in 1843, Osgood was named pastor of New York City's first Unitarian Church, the Church of the Messiah, in 1849, a position he held for two decades before taking orders in the Episcopal Church in 1870. For most of his years as a Unitarian, the Church of the Messiah was located on Broadway opposite Waverly Place in lower Manhattan, and so the Osgood family lived in a three-story, brick house on West Eleventh Street, within walking distance of the church.

In 1850, the year after his arrival in New York, Osgood traveled to Fairfield, Connecticut, to secure a summer residence, and the family spent the next few summers as boarders in this small, coastal village. In 1857 he bought the eight acres of land next to the cottage in which his family had been staying and built Mosswood, an eighteen-room house situated not far from the Fairfield train depot, yet within walking distance of the Long Island Sound. The property was said to have been a tract that "one would hardly accept as a gift, it scarcely being a sheep pasture for quality, overrun with cedars and cumbered with plenty of stones." Over the next twenty years, Osgood transformed this land into a showpiece of contemporary cottage design in the style of Andrew Jackson Downing, the nineteenth century's most influential landscape gardener and "apostle of taste."

Osgood created extensive gardens on the property, laid out winding sidewalks, dug a lily pool, built smaller summer houses around the main house, placed a half-size Italian statue of Dante on the grounds, and added many pine trees, planting one whenever he performed a baptism or marriage. According to one account, "the apparently worthless natural encumbrances upon the place he converted into ornaments. The stones and rocks made fences, recesses, grottoes, monuments, trellises, and landscape-finishings." Many of these rocks were carved with quotations from the Bible and from Osgood's favorite works of literature, as well as with the names of family members, classic poets, and Christian prophets. In a crowning gesture, Osgood built a gazebo-like structure out of cedar and placed it upon a high rock bordering the street. From this wooden pulpit, which came to be known as "Union Tower," Osgood preached occasional sermons during the Civil War to crowds gathered in the street below. Finally, in the year before his death, Osgood changed the name of the street on which Mosswood was located from *Cedar Street* to *Unquowa Road*, using the Indian name for *Fairfield*, which is said to mean "go further."

Soon after Mosswood was built, Osgood's youngest daughter Mabel Gray was born in New York City on 26 January 1859. Though she lived most of the year in the family's Greenwich Village home and attended Miss Lucy Green's school for girls at Number One Fifth Avenue, Wright received her true education at Mosswood. As she recalls in "The Story of a Garden" in *The Friendship of Nature*, "with my first consciousness, the days were filled with planting and with growth; the pines already hid the walls, and cattle tracks were widened into paths and wound among young maples, elms, and beeches. Then there grew in me a love that made the four garden walls seem like the boundaries of the world." She and her father, she once told an interviewer, "had splendid experiences, here in the garden in my girlhood."

Despite the obvious mutual affection that existed between father and daughter, Osgood's all-encompassing influence on his daughter's life affected her choice of career, partner in marriage, and place of residence in ways not always consistent with her desires. In a revealing aside during a late interview, Wright noted that she "intended to go to Cornell to study medicine, but I married instead," a statement that assumes added significance when juxtaposed with her father's thoughts on the matter, as stated in his essay "The Education of Daughters." "If young women wish to be lawyers, preachers, physicians, or merchants," Osgood wrote, "we would put no harsher obstacle before them than our honest opinion that such is not their providential career, whilst we would do everything in our power to throw open to their pursuit those spheres of action most congenial with their nature." Although he was a progressive, liberal thinker for his time, Wright's father remained committed to the notion of "separate spheres" for men and women and believed that good training would produce a daughter with "a disciplined, sagacious intellect without masculine hardness, delicate sensibility without imbecile listlessness, active energy without moping drudgery."

Swayed, no doubt, by her father's opinions about the proper occupation for a woman, Mabel married James Osborne Wright (1852–1920) on 25 September 1884. James, who appears as "Evan" in some of Mabel's novels, was a British bibliographer and rare book dealer whom Mabel had met through her father at one of the many fashionable art, print, and book sales held at Leavitt's in New York's Clinton Hall. In her autobiography, *My New York* (1926), Mabel describes James at this time as "a slight, tallish young fellow, usually dressed in tweed with a tailless Scotch cap set on somewhat awry, clean shaven save for an unusually curved mustache, very heavy brows and sea-gray blue eyes." He was also, she notes elsewhere, "if possible, even more absorbed in nature than I."

Writing Nature in New England

After a period of travel in Europe following their wedding, Mabel Wright and her new husband returned to the United States to take up

5

residence at the Osgood home in New York City, Mabel's father having died in 1880 at age sixty-seven. At the same time, they also retained Mosswood in Fairfield, from which James would commute to work in New York City on the train during the summer months. How Wright spent her first few years of marriage is largely undocumented, but one journalist noted that her "urge to write followed experiences of illness and social seclusion. Nature became her comrade, as well as her nurse that aroused new vitality." Wright once told an interviewer that "I think that my husband as well as my father expected me to become a writer. But when I would show him some of my efforts he would say: 'See here, Mab, these are green apples. Wait till they ripen a little.'" Despite such feeble encouragement, after six years of married life Wright began to publish nature essays anonymously in the *New York Times* and the *New York Evening Post*, keeping them a secret, at first, even from her husband. In 1925 she recounted the process by which these articles became her first published book:

> Edmund Clarence Stedman, who was a close friend of us all, strongly urged when he heard of the articles, that they should appear in book form. Other articles were added to those published, and the whole was submitted to George P. Brett, a friend of my husband's, who was then, as he is now, president of MacMillan's. They appeared in April, 1894.
>
> Nature books were quite a novelty at that time, and "Friendship of Nature" as this volume was called, was a great success. My husband was just as much delighted with its success as I was.

Sometime that same year, James Wright also published his wife's translation of *The Bibliomaniac*, a short story by Charles Nodier, in a small-press edition of 150 copies. In her husband's eyes, Wright's apples had finally ripened.

Wright's work was also a success in the eyes of British and American critics, who generally praised *The Friendship of Nature* for its poetic language and accurate representation of the local landscape. "The writer has a sympathetic eye and touch for every face that nature wears in her New England home," said the *Dial*. "These graceful sketches reflect the changing aspects of the blooming and the waning year, and convince us that the author, though writing prose, is a true poet in the Emersonian sense, namely, in the power to see the miraculous in the common." "Whether we like the author's treatment of flowers or birds the better we do not know," admitted the *New York Times*, "for both subjects are delicately handled. . . . The lady is always in touch."

Wright also received a letter from Oliver Wendell Holmes, whom she had quoted in the book, thanking her for her "charming little book which shall go into my shelves by the side of [Gilbert] White's '[Natural History of] Selbourne' [1789]." Likewise, the reviewer for the *Philadelphia Evening Bulletin* found "much of the feeling of Henry D. Thoreau between the covers of this book."

Some of the most appreciative readers of *Friendship* were the other women writers of Wright's day. "I know of nothing but Alphonse Karr's 'Tour Round My Garden' [1855] with which to compare it," wrote Harriet Prescott Spofford in a letter to Wright. "I was particularly interested in the 'Story of a Garden,'—but there is not a page without its charm. It is a book that not only must have made you happy in the living and the writing, but which will bring the out-door world into the life of many a house-bound reader." Frances Theodora Parsons, whose popular *How to Know the Wild Flowers* (1893) was also written in Fairfield, expressed similar sentiments about the book. "I have read it all through and have found it really delightful. It seems to me charmingly written and full of thought and affection. The illustrations are peculiarly satisfactory. They seem to get at the very heart of the different spots. I do not believe you can fail to meet with a real success, dear Mrs. Wright, and I congratulate you most heartily."

As Parsons's comments suggest, one aspect of Wright's work that has largely been ignored is her photography. Wright's photographs not only accompanied the text of *The Friendship of Nature* and many of her other books but also appeared in the works of other writers, including Katherine M. Abbott, Frank Samuel Child, Alice Morse Earl, and Lena May McCauley. One contemporary described her as a "skilled amateur photographer," a designation that did not even exist until the late 1870s when the dry glass plate was first marketed. In fact, Wright was one of a number of leisure-class women who found the dry-plate process so accommodating that they continued to use the plates even after the introduction in 1888 of George Eastman's Kodak, which used flexible roll film. Typically, Wright would transport her tripod, large-view camera, and glass plates around the Fairfield area by horse and buggy and then develop her negatives upon her return home. In all, she was able to make more than four hundred negatives of various subjects, including bathers in the Long Island Sound, activities at local cider mills, and many scenic landscapes around her home and garden.

In her photographs almost as much as in her writings, Wright reveals her anxiety about the changes occurring to the Connecticut landscape during her lifetime. Whereas her father could in 1877 proclaim the benefits of country life in Fairfield by noting that the village "does not grow much, if any," by 1923 (when eye problems prevented Wright from taking any more pictures) Osgood's "quiet old village" had become a busy suburb of nearby Bridgeport, the state's leading industrial city. One of Wright's responses to these developments was to experiment with "colonial revival" photos in a manner later popularized by Wallace Nutting. Rather than travel the necessary half hour to find photographic subjects in Bridgeport's bustling business district, Wright chose instead to recreate scenes from Fairfield's past, using costumed models posed in and around colonial buildings, as a kind of bulwark against the post-Victorian world. In a similar form of nostalgia for preindustrial life, she mounted many of her landscapes on heavy boards and provided them with pastoral titles, such as "Sheepfold" and "Evening Shadows."

This romantic nostalgia contrasts sharply with Wright's approach in her field guides, in which she increasingly came to employ the techniques of modern science to identify and describe birds and plants accurately. Until about 1890, as Wright observed in the *Critic*, "it was well-nigh impossible to obtain any inexpensive handbooks upon birds, flowers, trees, stars, or any other of the objects that set the Nature lover's mind at work, that were at once accurate and yet written in a style suited to popular consumption." Wright's second book, *Birdcraft* (1895), helped fill this gap by providing a catalog of birds arranged in taxonomic order, along with descriptions of each species' appearance, song, and behavior, followed by brief essays of personal observation and anecdote. One of the earliest inexpensive field guides to birds, *Birdcraft* was hailed by the naturalist John Burroughs as "a readable and interesting book" in an 1895 letter to Wright. "I wish I could have had the help of such a book when I began my bird studies," Burroughs told her. "I shall take pleasure in recommending it to persons who write me for the name of a handy and reliable book on our birds." Others clearly shared Burroughs's enthusiasm, as *Birdcraft* was reprinted nine times, the last in 1936, and was eclipsed only by the appearance of Roger Tory Peterson's *Field Guide to the Birds* in 1934.

Much of Wright's research for *Birdcraft* was based on her observations of bird behavior in Fairfield, but she also drew on her ornithological studies during the winters of 1893 and 1894 at the American

Museum of Natural History in New York City, where she received assistance from curator Joel A. Allen and his assistant, Frank Chapman. Wright's letters to Allen show her to be both appreciative of his help and self-deprecating about her own ornithological authority. "Please remember that I consider it a great favor ... for you to trouble to help me at all," Wright wrote to him on 11 May 1894. In October, after Allen published a positive review of *The Friendship of Nature* in *The Auk*, the scientific journal of the American Ornithologists' Union, Wright told him she was "very, very much pleased by the notice itself in such a magazine, but more so that you thought the book deserving of the kindness with which you treated it." The following March, she again thanked Allen for his "wonderful" revision of her proof and expressed her fear that "without it ... *The Auk* would have stuck its beak into the book and rent it asunder." In the same letter Wright also asked Allen to tell Chapman that "if he has a chance to say a word for 'Birdcraft' [at a reception for the American Academy of Sciences] and wishes to be satirical he can describe it as being 'sentimental & harmless,'" an indication of her awareness of the challenges facing women who sought recognition from a mostly male scientific establishment.

Both *Birdcraft* and its companion guide to plant life, *Flowers and Ferns in Their Haunts* (1901), reflect Wright's growing awareness not only of science but also of the increasing threats to plant habitat and animal populations in the decades before and after the turn of the twentieth century. Birds in particular were being hunted to extinction for sport, for the market, and by hunters employed by milliners, who used the parts, skins, and feathers of the birds to decorate women's hats. Outraged by these abuses, Wright became active in the conservation movement in the late 1890s, and her writings during these years reflected her deepening commitment to the cause. In *Birdcraft*, for instance, she notes that "not only is the wild bird a part of the inheritance of the people, but the people are the trustees of its liberty." And in *Flowers and Ferns in Their Haunts* she reminds readers that "wild flowers taken from their surroundings and considered as aggregations of calyx, corolla, stamen, and pistil are wholly different from the same flowers seen in their native haunts. ... The wild flower and fern is only to be truly known where it creeps, clings, or sways untroubled in its home."

During this same period, Wright began working as a nature educator, writing fact-filled books for children and hosting a group of neighborhood students at her home for an informal bird class. Though Wright herself had no children, she took great interest in the education of young people, an occupation of which her father certainly would have approved. "The out-door school is the best for the little ones," he wrote in *Mile Stones in Our Life-Journey* (rev. ed., 1877), "and the true kindergarten is under the trees with the real objects about them to name and study." Teaching such a bird class was also in line with the "nature study" movement being advocated by Liberty Hyde Bailey, dean of the College of Agriculture at Cornell University, who encouraged educators not only to introduce students to the natural sciences through books but also to take them outside where they could "put the pupil in a sympathetic attitude toward nature for the purpose of increasing the joy of living." For her 1897 bird class, Wright read chapters from her *Citizen Bird* (1897) and took the children on field trips to nearby natural areas. She also borrowed various stuffed birds from Frank Chapman at the American Museum of Natural History, perched these birds about her garden, and asked the children to locate and identify each species.

In her children's books, Wright attempted to achieve a mix of fact and fiction that was faithful to scientific truth but fanciful enough to keep the attention of young readers. Two of her early books—*Tommy-Anne and the Three Hearts* (1896) and *Wabeno, the Magician* (1899), a sequel—constitute "one of the most ambitious works of nature fiction for children published in the nineteenth century—and also one of the best," according to Robert Henry Welker. Two of her other children's books feature the work of well-known collaborators. *Citizen Bird*, a bird book for beginners, was written with Elliott Coues and illustrated by Louis Agassiz Fuertes, and *Four-Footed Americans and Their Kin* (1898), a sequel to *Citizen Bird*, was edited by Frank Chapman and illustrated by Ernest Thompson Seton. Although all of these works employ anthropomorphism, they are not anthropocentric, and Wright took particular care to ensure readers that she did not go beyond the bounds of verifiable facts when depicting the behavior of her nonhuman characters—a particularly sensitive issue at the time, given her vocal criticism of such "nature fakers" as William J. Long. As she noted in *Tommy-Anne and the Three Hearts*, "The lives and habits of plants and animals, however fancifully treated in this book, are in strict accordance with the known facts of their existence." For her contribution to the advancement of science in these and other works, Wright was named an associate member of the American Ornithologists' Union in 1895 and a member in 1901.

Wright's transition into adult fiction, which would yield a prolific run of ten works of fiction in twelve years, began with a suggestion from George Brett, following the British publication of Mary Annette Beauchamp Russell's *Elizabeth and Her German Garden* (1898). "Mr. Brett suggested that I write an American garden story [in a] Similar Vein," Wright later recalled. "He and I decided to keep this new venture in the field of adult fiction separate from my children and nature books and so when 'The Garden of a Commuter's Wife' appeared [in 1901], it was under the pseudonym of 'Barbara.'" Thus began her series of semiautobiographical "Barbara" books, which kept readers guessing for five years as to their authorship. When "Barbara's" identity was finally revealed in 1906 by Jeanette Gilder of the *Critic* and Francis Halsey of the *New York Times*, Wright says she "continued to write all sorts of things, but without that joyous unselfconsciousness and freedom an anonymous author enjoys." According to the *Bookman*, however, "Wright's anonymity was at best half-anonymity. Almost everybody in touch with literary and publishing circles [was] quite aware of the author's identity from the first."

Why Wright eventually chose to abandon nonfiction nature writing is unclear, but one of the appeals of fiction writing must have been that it allowed her to call upon her personal experiences without having to adhere to literal truth. Wright never completely turned her back on her garden, though, as most of her "Barbara" books are hybrid texts, mixing discussions of nature and tips on gardening with diary entries, letters, and sketches. Half of her fictional works are more conventional novels, but these are much less successful and suffer from contrived circumstances, undeveloped characters, and stilted speech. As the *New York Times* commented about her 1909 novel *Poppea of the Post Office*, "better a week in the garden with Barbara than a cycle of plot with Mrs. Wright." Despite their weaknesses, many of Wright's fictional works offer valuable glimpses of her views on urban and suburban issues, social patterns among the upper classes, and the struggles of women to adapt to changing expectations in public and private life.

The Most Influential Woman in the Audubon Movement
Wright's choice of title for her collaboration with Elliott Coues— *Citizen Bird*—suggests another means by which she sought to protect

threatened plant and animal species: civic activism. As Paul Brooks has noted in *Speaking for Nature* (1980), Wright was "an early exponent of the doctrine that all living creatures, not just human beings, had their natural rights." She not only corresponded with such naturalists as William Brewster, John Burroughs, Olive Thorne Miller, and Florence Merriam Bailey, but she also became known to many conservationists through her work with the Audubon Society on both the state and national levels.

After the first Audubon Society folded in 1888, just two years after its creation by George Bird Grinnell, the Audubon movement was revived in 1896, when state societies formed in Massachusetts and Pennsylvania. These were followed in 1897 by groups in New York, New Hampshire, Illinois, Maine, Wisconsin, New Jersey, Rhode Island, and the District of Columbia. The Connecticut Audubon Society grew out of a class in Parliamentary Law held by the Eunice Dennie Burr Chapter of the Daughters of the American Revolution (D.A.R.) in Fairfield. As Wright explained in a 1923 article, "for drill in organization, the technique of forming a society was rehearsed and it was called, for the sake of a name, The Audubon Society." The drill became reality when, on 28 January 1898, Wright and twelve other women assembled at the home of Helen Glover in Fairfield to officially form the Audubon Society of Connecticut (now the Connecticut Audubon Society). Wright traveled to Fairfield from New York City specifically for this meeting and was elected president of the society, a position she retained for twenty-six years, during which time she was the driving force behind most of its activities.

The first annual report of the society suggests the variety of causes its membership espoused: "The purpose of the Society is to discourage the purchase or use of the feathers of any birds for ornamentation, except those of the ostrich and domesticated fowl, and game birds used as food. . . . Members shall discourage the destruction of birds and their eggs, and do all in their power to protect them. . . . Members shall use their influence to establish 'Bird-Day' in the schools of the State of Connecticut in connection with Arbor-Day, and do all in their power to encourage the study of Natural History." During its first years of existence, membership in the Connecticut society grew rapidly. In its fourth year alone, the organization grew by 1,565 members, many of whom were school children whose membership fees had been

waived. Wright had mounted an aggressive program of youth education, which included sending a Bird-Day program to 1,350 Connecticut schools, preparing slide lectures on such topics as "The Birds
about Home" and "The Adventures of a Robin," purchasing a parlor
stereopticon for projection of these lantern slides, and distributing
bird charts and circulating libraries of natural history books to needy
schools and libraries. Other activities of the society included petition-
ing state and local legislatures, distributing bird brochures to farmers,
and making contacts with other groups that had similar goals.

Wright was keenly aware of the many demands placed on women
who chose to enter the public sphere through such local action. Defending the secretaries of the various state Audubon societies in 1902,
Wright seemed to be speaking as much about herself as about them
when she announced: "Be it here understood that many of the most
active of these secretaries are women with family cares, who conduct a
correspondence that amounts to a business wholly without pay." Similarly, when her sister Agnes, who had been caring for their mother in
the family's Eleventh Street home in New York City, was struck with
"nervous prostration" in 1905, Wright told Frank Chapman that she
"flatly refused to run that big house and see after mother both, as it
would end my work of writing forever." She repeated her preference
for professional obligations over domestic duties when she wrote to
Audubon leader T. Gilbert Pearson in 1913 after a period of illness:
"I'm picking up again but feel that I must concentrate my work in [the]
future to what really counts, and let society and inane visiting go,
together with many things which the Devil of modern life has invented
to kill both time and the people who follow him."

At the same moment as she was directing the progress of the Audubon Society of Connecticut, Wright was also becoming involved with
the National Association of Audubon Societies (now the National
Audubon Society). As president of one of the state societies, Wright
automatically became a member of the National Committee upon its
founding in 1901 and of the Board of Directors of the National
Association upon its incorporation in 1905. When she finally resigned
from the Board in 1928, the remaining members informed her that
"the unanimous feeling was that this Association, the subject of ornithology, and the cause of conservation of wild life all owe to you the
deepest debt of gratitude for your services in the field of natural

history during the past thirty years." T. Gilbert Pearson also personally offered his "undying gratitude for [her] . . . friendship, loyalty, and support" over the years.

Wright had become "the most influential woman in the Audubon movement," according to Oliver H. Orr Jr., in part because for almost three years prior to the formation of the National Committee she had edited the Audubon department of *Bird-Lore*, a bimonthly magazine founded by Frank Chapman in February 1899 to function as a popular alternative to *The Auk*. Chapman was the sole owner, publisher, and editor of *Bird-Lore* for its first thirty-six years, and the magazine was a private venture throughout his tenure, but *Bird-Lore* maintained many financial and editorial links to the Audubon movement. For the magazine's first eleven years, Wright assisted Chapman as associate editor, and she remained an active contributor until her death. From 1899 to 1906 she edited the Audubon department, writing opinion pieces in support of bird conservation and contributing articles about the habits and haunts of various species; from 1907 to 1910 she edited the school department, where she continued her campaign to educate young people about birds by preparing pamphlets, sponsoring contests, and encouraging teachers to organize Audubon chapters in the schools; and after 1910 she served as a contributing editor, writing occasional articles but having no direct editorial responsibilities. In his *Autobiography of a Bird-Lover* (1933), written the year before Wright's death, Chapman called her assistance "invaluable."

In the first few, critical years of *Bird-Lore*'s publication, Wright articulated a coherent strategy for environmental reform in her regular column in the Audubon department. To effect cultural change, she argued, Audubon members must pursue a dual agenda of education and legislation. "To introduce people to the bird in the bush is the way to create a public sentiment to keep it there, and to make it possible to obtain legislative authority for the enactment and keeping of good bird laws, which are the backbone of protection," Wright informed the readers of *Bird-Lore*'s first issue. She repeated this claim in the magazine's second issue, noting that "the only way to do permanent good is, on one side, to educate the moral nature so that it will not desire to do the wrong act, and on the other to work for the establishment and *enforcement* of laws that shall punish those who do the wrong."

Throughout the issues of *Bird-Lore*, Wright time and again emphasized the need for the female membership of the early Audubon movement to refrain from basing their appeals solely on sentiment. "At a time when a great majority look askance at the startling array of societies that they are asked to 'join,' it behooves all Bird Protective bodies to conduct themselves with extreme conservatism, that they may not bear the stigma of being called emotional 'fads,' but really appeal to those whom they seek to interest," she stated in "The Conducting of Audubon Societies," an 1899 column. "Many men (and women also) have many minds, and a form of appeal that will attract one will repel another. It is upon the tactful management of these appeals and the bringing of the subject vitally home to different classes and ages, that the life of the Audubon Societies depends." The need for emotional "conservatism" was a frequent refrain of Wright in these early years. "Be the roads many—illustrated lectures to arouse public sentiment, birdless bonnets, leaflets, thousands of pledge cards signed by ready sympathizers—the goal must be conservative, well thought out legislation, free from any taint of emotional insanity," she wrote in another 1899 column, titled "The Law and the Bird." Putting the matter more plainly the next year, she reminded her readers that "in all reform movements, especially those where sense and sentiment are interwoven, there is but a step from the sublime to the very, very ridiculous." Emotionalism, according to Wright, runs the risk of lapsing into exaggeration and thereby alienating potential advocates. As a result, she wrote in 1903, "Audubon workers should realize their responsibility, the importance of accuracy, and keep themselves well-informed,—as there is nothing so disastrous as the effect of loose statements and overdrawn claims upon the skeptical."

Making good on her call for a dual agenda of education and legislation, Wright and the Connecticut society managed over the years to support a wide range of legislative initiatives, including presenting a bird bill in the state legislature in 1901; successfully lobbying for the enactment of a hunter's license law and non-spring shooting law in 1907; passing a resolution favoring the establishment of national forest reserves in the Southern Appalachians and the White Mountains in 1908, and encouraging other state societies to take similar action; lobbying for the passage of a state bill curbing and regulating the taking of birds and eggs by collectors in 1911; working to protect sandpipers and recognize starlings as an alien species in 1912; pushing for the passage of the Migratory Bird Treaty Act (1918) in 1916 and 1917; protesting against the offer of a bounty for bald eagles in Alaska with a circular letter sent to all the state Audubon societies and all the state boards of agriculture in 1919 and 1920; and lobbying in 1924 for the expansion of Sequoia National Park.

Building Birdcraft Sanctuary

Involved as she was with such state and national issues, Wright was most successful in her efforts at the local level, as can be seen in her development of a local songbird sanctuary and museum, the first such facility owned and governed by a state Audubon society. As early as 1901 Wright had been calling for the creation of "song bird reservations," arguing in the pages of *Bird-Lore* that "the day has passed when it is enough to satisfy the demands for bird protection by simply ceasing to kill." By 1910 she had grown even more insistent about the need for such places, noting that "every day the cities and manufacturing towns are growing more solidly packed with human beings; the outlying brush lots and woodland being stripped for fuel, and the many other uses of wood, while the land itself is taking on a prohibitory value. Now is the time to secure these oases in what may be called the desert of civilization. In many places it is now or never." In February 1914, after Wright and a group of Fairfield residents attended *Sanctuary*, a masque about the conversion of a plume hunter to a bird protectionist, the interest in creating a local sanctuary reached its peak. The masque, written by Percy Mackaye and staged at the Astor Place Theater in New York City, had originally been performed in 1913 for the dedication of the Helen Woodruff Smith Bird Sanctuary, operated by the Bird Club of Meriden, New Hampshire, and the residents of Fairfield no doubt found themselves spurred into action by the achievements of this rival group.

Annie Burr Jennings, a prominent Fairfield resident and heiress to the Standard Oil fortune, provided the funding for the sanctuary's purchase, but Wright was clearly the driving force behind its creation and the selection of its site. In the minutes of the society, Wright was careful to defer all credit for the donation of the property to Jennings, claiming that "not only was it entirely spontaneous upon the part of the donor but absolutely unsolicited." Wright's many published opinions, however, as well as the recollections of an Audubon Society member, suggest that the idea for the sanctuary was neither spontaneous nor unsolicited but the culmination of Wright's long interest in bird protection and public education. "Mrs. Wright was very anxious to have some such sanctuary," recalled Audubon society member Deborah Glover, "and persuaded Miss Annie B. Jennings to donate it."

After examining two sites, a hundred-acre plot distant from town and a ten-acre tract close to Main Street, Wright and Jennings decided upon the smaller, more accessible one in 1914, and Jennings purchased and deeded the land to the Audubon Society of Connecticut. Named after Wright's 1895 book *Birdcraft*, the sanctuary was established on a calf pasture that perfectly embodied Wright's ideal landscape for a protected natural area: a "wild untilled land, where leaves have fallen year on year and gone to decay and dead wood been left where it fell." Because the site was also located directly across the street from Mosswood, Wright was able to supervise closely the sanctuary's development, including the erection of a cat-proof fence, the building of stone gate posts, the construction of a bungalow for the caretaker and a museum for exhibitions, the cutting of trails, the dredging of a pond, and the building of birdbaths and birdhouses. Perhaps most important, Wright directed the planting of indigenous trees and shrubs to encourage the ecological well-being of the birds, an idea that has since come to be known as "birdscaping."

As it grew from vision to reality, Birdcraft Sanctuary became a model for local wildlife and habitat preservation efforts throughout the United States. Frank Chapman, writing in *Bird-Lore* in 1915, described the sanctuary as "an object lesson in conservation and museum methods": "In its own field of local bird-life, Birdcraft Sanctuary promises to render a greater and more effective return for the capital invested than can be shown by any museum in this country. One cannot say by any similar institution for we know of none like it.... Ten acres cannot harbor many birds nor a little museum in the country be seen by a large number of people ... but the idea which they embody can reach to the ends of the earth." Helen Glover, secretary of the Connecticut society, noted in her annual report for 1917–18 that the sanctuary had hosted visitors from Seattle, California, and Cornell University, and in September 1923, when Edith Roosevelt was seeking an appropriate memorial for her late husband, the former first lady traveled to Fairfield, ate lunch with Wright, and "went over the Sanctuary in every detail," noting its beauty and the economy of its management. The result of this and other meetings was the twelve-acre Theodore Roosevelt Memorial Sanctuary in Oyster Bay, Long Island, a direct descendent of Wright's work at Birdcraft.

Modern conservationists might recoil in horror at the style of wild-life management practiced at Birdcraft in these early years, but the removal of so-called "problem species" from songbird sanctuaries was common practice at the beginning of the twentieth century. In a 1922 letter to Wright from Frederic C. Walcott, president of the Connecticut State Board of Fisheries and Game, Walcott gave Wright "a kind of blanket permission to use your own judgment within the boundaries of your sanctuary and on your own grounds and destroy anything that you think detrimental to the purpose of your sanctuary. . . . I would not hesitate officially or otherwise to encourage the killing of English sparrows, starlings, crows, Cooper and sharp shinned hawks, wandering house cats, weasels, rats, red squirrels, occasionally jays, and even chip monks when caught in the act." In the first three years of the sanctuary's existence, its caretaker killed 524 European starlings, 269 English sparrows, 28 purple grackles, and 12 crows, and trapped 14 northern shrikes, 4 sparrow hawks, 4 sharp-shinned hawks, 3 Cooper's hawks, 3 red-shouldered hawks, 2 long-eared owls, 1 barred owl, and 1 screech owl (releasing only the owls and the red-shouldered hawks). In addition, 107 cats were taken, along with 21 rats, 17 striped snakes, 1 skunk, and 1 weasel.

Wright's concern about protecting native birds from "problem species" parallels her arguments in *Bird-Lore* about the threat to songbirds from uneducated, insensitive immigrants, particularly those from central and southern Europe. "In appealing to the average child of the public school," Wright claimed in an 1899 column, "it should be remembered of how many races this average child is compounded,—races with instincts concerning what are called lower animals, quite beyond the moral comprehension of the animal-loving Anglo-Saxon." Likewise, in a later column regarding the posting of game laws, Wright expressed concern about the inability of English-language materials to reach "the newly arrived foreign element unable to read English who, together with cats, are the birds' worst enemies." Unfortunately, Wright's nativism was shared by many early conservationists and nature enthusiasts, including Andrew Jackson Downing, Henry Fairfield Osborn, and Madison Grant. As Thomas R. Dunlap acknowledges, nature study was "most popular among the descendants of the pioneers—the white, 'Anglo-Saxon,' Protestant people who dominated American society—and their commitment was in part an effort to preserve their culture and its virtues in a new world." Native species, therefore, symbolized both an affirmation of the Western European roots of American culture and a resistance to the new influx of immigrants from foreign lands. Landscape historian John Stilgoe has posed the question in this way: "If immigrant birds drove out native species, . . . might not immigrant people overwhelm Americans of English, German, and Irish descent, Americans already weakened by stressful urban lives given over to business?"

Apart from Wright's nativist assumptions and invasive management practices, the basic argument behind the creation of Birdcraft Sanctuary and Museum remains compelling. From its founding the sanctuary sought to integrate a nonanthropocentric philosophy about songbirds with a community-based nature center intended for the education of children and adults alike. Wright outlined the first part of this mission in 1915 when she wrote that "the Song Bird Sanctuary . . . is an oasis in a desert of material things. In it the bird may lead its own life for that life's sake, and the joy of many such lives overflows all arbitrary boundaries in its ethical benefit to the community and state." "At Birdcraft," she added later, "we do not seek to humanize birds, or to tame them artificially; we try to look at their lives from their own angle, not ours."

The second, educational part of the sanctuary's mission quickly became a difficult task when the songbirds were driven away by the popularity of the sanctuary itself. As a result, the Board of Governors had to restrict admission to the sanctuary proper (a practice since discontinued) and bolster the offerings in the museum. One benefit of this decision was the mounting of a "Birds of Connecticut" exhibition, a collection Wright found to be "of greater value to the student than would be a much larger but mixed collection. Such a local group clarifies the mind about the birds of home and is an introduction to study of a wider scope."

This intimate, regional focus is perhaps the most significant aspect of Birdcraft's mission. Unlike large national parks and wildlife preserves, which often appear unconnected to the communities that surround them, Birdcraft has been a familiar feature on the Fairfield landscape since the sanctuary's inception. As one commentator noted in the early twentieth century, "it is passing strange that such a place should have remained to this day in a wild state within easy hearing of the rumbling New Haven road's trains and in sight of the thousands of automobiles that pass that way." Wright herself had proposed keeping the sanctuary close to the railroad station and Main Street for this very reason—so "that those of us who know the land from sea to hills may have before us a bit of what was and the younger generation in its turn feel its inspiration also."

In 1957, however, when the state government announced that the Connecticut Turnpike was to be constructed through nearly half of the sanctuary's land, Birdcraft became a case study in the difficulty of preserving open space within a rapidly growing community. "The first offer made by the State Highway Department was for $20,000," noted the Connecticut Audubon Society's secretary in June of 1957. "This offer has been increased to $32,000—the top appraisal. None of these appraisals took into consideration the value of land as a Sanctuary, but considered only the real estate value." Eventually the society received $45,000 in compensation from the state, but the money could not begin to account for the loss of more than 40 percent of Birdcraft's total acreage.

Despite its reduction in size, and the now-constant hum of the thruway to its north, Birdcraft has remained an active facility of the Connecticut Audubon Society, although the society relocated its offices to bigger quarters in 1971. In part because of its ability to survive as a kind of living example of Wright's own determination, Birdcraft was added to the National Register of Historic Places in 1982 and registered as a National Historic Landmark in 1993.

A Fitting Memorial

To the end of her life, Wright remained involved in various writing and conservation projects, but the loss of her husband in 1920 devastated her so thoroughly that Birdcraft seemed to be her "only pleasure left." In a letter to T. Gilbert Pearson in October of that year, Wright said, "I have been down and out all summer, for the shock of the loss of my companion in *everything*, for thirty five years, aside from the sudden going has been too much for me. Now I am striving to make a life through such work as I may be able to do without too much *physical* exertion, Audubon work, writing, book chooser for our town library &c." By 1916 the couple sold Mosswood and built Oakhaven, a smaller, eight-room cottage across the street, but by 1922 even this dwelling became too difficult for Wright to maintain on her own, and she moved into a nearby cottage, known as The Little Brown House on the Hill. In 1922 she also began to experience heart difficulties and eye trouble, problems reflected in the title of her 1925 essay "A Tired Woman's Roses." Initially Wright had planned to publish a historical romance based upon the life of her grand-aunt, Susanna Haswell Rowson, author of *Charlotte Temple* (1791), but in her last years she was able to produce only three additional works: *My New York* (1926), her autobiography; *Captains of the Watch of Life and Death* (1927), a book about nurses and patients; and *Eudora's Men* (1931), a novel that traces a New England family from the Civil War to World War I. As a final tribute to Wright before her death, the Connecticut women's board of the 1926 Sesqui-Centennial Exposition in Philadelphia named her Connecticut's outstanding woman literary figure. She died at age seventy-five, on 16 July 1934, and was buried at Oaklawn Cemetery in Fairfield beside her husband.

One of Wright's comments from *The Friendship of Nature* may well serve as a fitting memorial to the message of this forgotten writer and conservationist, whose remarkable legacy lies before us still. "If we only knew it all, knew all that there is to learn between the coming and going! The journey is so short, and before we are thoroughly used to being here, the time has come for our flitting. If only, like the birds, we may keep in our hearts the songs of another season!"

THE FRIENDSHIP OF NATURE

As its full title suggests, *The Friendship of Nature: A New England Chronicle of Birds and Flowers* features three major themes: the observation of species over time ("chronicle" is from the Greek for time, *khronos*), the significance of regionalism, and the nature of friendship. Likewise, Thomas J. Lyon has argued that "the literature of nature has three main dimensions to it: natural history information, personal responses to nature, and philosophical interpretation of nature." Because Wright's three major themes map so closely onto the main dimensions of nature writing as defined by Lyon, it is worth briefly examining the ways in which *The Friendship of Nature* is representative of its genre, a form of writing now undergoing a renaissance reminiscent of the "back-to-nature" movement a century ago.

The Friendship of Nature consists of eleven related chapters whose central purpose is the presentation of natural history information, a task Wright accomplishes by the detailed observation of nature over time. Like many works of nature writing, the book is organized roughly around the passage of the seasons, taking the reader from May Day in spring through summer, fall, and winter. Wright follows this same seasonal progression in other texts, and her decision to arrange her work in this manner suggests a purpose larger than the obvious parallel with the progress of the calendar. In contrast to Thoreau's *Walden*, which concludes with a meditation on the renewal of life in spring, *Friendship* ends with the observation that the attention devoted to the warm seasons can bring equal rewards in the cold, "for the tones of winter are as really distinctive as those of all other seasons. If you search, as you have done each day, in the spring, summer, or autumn, you will find constantly a new beauty, a fresh surprise" (131).

By guiding the reader through the seasons in this fashion, Wright not only reveals the hidden qualities of the winter months but also reminds the reader of the constancy of ecological change and, from that, draws larger conclusions about the nature of life:

> A morning in winter; can there be morning in the dead season? There is no dead season. Men say that it is summer, or autumn, or winter, but Nature has set no fixed bounds to her actions, and does not perish when she casts off her apparel, but, gathering her forces to herself, prepares for new effort. Nature knows but two changes, putting forth and withdrawing, and between these there is a constant transition. We call the first of them birth, the last, death, and choose to surround them with mystery. Nature, left to herself, has gentle gradations, blending all from the first breath to the last, as she mingles the prismatic colours, with no gap to measure where youth ends or age begins. We fasten attributes to things, and hold them there by mere persistency. There is really no dead season; there are no snows so deep but somewhere in the firs the crossbill holds his sign of the sacred legend, no ice so thick but under it the warm current stirs, no age so dreary that love may not quicken it until eternal spring. (129–30)

As these comments suggest, Wright's observations of nature clearly extend beyond the literal facts to embrace the figurative and metaphorical. "We cannot all be positive scientists," she notes, "and heaven help the world if we could be! The spirit of things would be dried away by letter, and the affections ranged in systems about material suns" (86). Yet *The Friendship of Nature* is no romantic reverie; rather, it is a scientifically informed description of a landscape in motion. As *Popular Science Monthly* noted upon the book's publication, "Even though repudiated, science has informed much of the book with beauty." Wright's extensive botanical and ornithological knowledge is apparent throughout the volume, particularly as she monitors the migration patterns and feeding habits of the birds. Observing the avian activity along her lane walk, for instance, Wright notes that "here the hermit thrush comes in May, and in October returns to feed on the wedge-shaped magnolia berries. Here the brown thrasher scratches and rustles daily and the wood thrush stays to nest, while the olive-backed and gray-cheeked thrushes make semi-annual visits. The catbird and the sociable robin find the lane too dull except for noon siestas, but the warblers love it for the shelter and the food it yields them" (99–100).

One seeming weakness of Wright's prose is her tendency to lapse into a Linnaean catalog of all the birds, flowers, trees, and other natural objects she encounters, a practice that may derive from her immersion in the research for *Birdcraft*, her handbook of New England birds, the same year she published *Friendship*. Wright displays her own awareness of this tendency in "Rustling Wings," where she notes during the fall migration of birds that "to catalogue each one would be reviewing New England ornithology" (110). Seen from another perspective, though, Wright's penchant for inclusion over exclusion is less an accident of circumstance than an integral part of her "New England Chronicle of Birds and Flowers," the unspoken argument of which is the need for integration of the personal and the regional. Contemporary nature writers articulate a similar message: to know *who* you are, you must know *where* you are; the narrative of place implies a deepening and extending of self through contact with nature, an extension of the self in space and time.

Wright makes this point explicitly in a later essay, inviting the reader to "come into the country with me, to *my* country, . . . I say *my* country, because it is only that from which one absorbs and in return yields personality, that deepest satisfaction may be had." In *The Friendship of Nature*, therefore, her record of the comings and goings of birds and the appearance and disappearance of wildflowers is best seen not as a dry catalog of scientific names but as a regional chronicle in the deepest sense: an extended account of events that helps Wright and her readers root themselves to the land. That Wright chooses to monitor the arrival and departure of *migratory* birds further emphasizes her attachment to the region. As John Holman, who succeeded Wright as president of the Connecticut Audubon Society, once noted,

"No one knew the older Fairfield better than she. Every road and woodland stream—every wild nook—every hill and meadow—all were to her places of enduring charm."

Given her father's occupation, it should come as no surprise that Wright may have modeled her chronicle after the Bible, and in particular after its attempt to make the land sacred through story. Stories shape our interaction with the land, providing ways of seeing and giving meaning to events that "take place" in particular locations. The land on which Wright resided, of course, had a long history of inhabitation before the arrival of Europeans, but most of these native stories were unavailable to Wright, as she acknowledged in a 1905 lecture about colonial history: "It is to be deeply regretted that the tradition and folk-lore of the Indian tribes native to the region have not been better preserved. The Pequots were exterminated literally before they were known, and the nomenclature of our rivers, etc., is little understood." In the absence of a native tradition, Wright turned to the stories with which she was most familiar—ancient mythology and the legacy of women's experience—in an attempt to foster a connection between herself and the land. As she informs the reader at the beginning of her text, the trail through her garden is "a much-trodden path in a long-discovered country, but each one discovers anew when he first sees it for himself" (31).

These two narrative traditions provide distinct yet complementary ways to understand the landscape of Wright's Connecticut. On the one hand, Wright uses ancient mythology to suggest that her relationship with nature is "timeless" or beyond time, a conception that also reinforces the cyclical, seasonal structure of her book. The opening of *Friendship*, in which Wright introduces the reader to the legend of the months of the year, is the most visible example of this strategy, as it provides a mythological explanation for the "strange contradiction" that makes the month of May feel more like April (35). On the other hand, Wright's references to a tradition of female engagement with the landscape suggest a specific, time-bound relationship linking the women of New England both to each other and to the natural world. In a sheltered nook Wright finds "the little white violets that our grandmothers cherished" (31); she instructs her reader to "fill your basket, your hat, your upturned gown" with roses (49); and she recalls the young women who, rose leaves in their aprons, turned to their mothers for the potpourri recipe, only to hear the words of their grandmothers' recipes being read (50). Annette Kolodny, Vera Norwood, and other ecofeminist literary critics have discussed the subtle ways in which American women have turned their intimacy with nature into a source of power, and Wright is very much a participant in this tradition of female empowerment. By the second paragraph of her book she is already asserting her authority over the male poets of New England, noting specifically that "the fringed gentian, set by Bryant in frayed and barren fields, frosty and solitary, usually follows the cardinal flower, in late September" (31).

Wright's most notable stylistic technique, her use of the second person, is both a product and source of this intimacy. "Come into the garden," Wright announces, offering the reader a personal invitation to join her on her walk, as well as a reminder to pay close attention along the way (31). She uses this technique especially well when describing transitions from one environment into another, when one's sensory awareness is heightened and some form of revelation is likely. When moving from orchard to woodland in "When Orchards Bloom," she tells the reader, "Go further yet into the wood; the banks grow steep, the road winds through a glen to the side of a narrow river, which tumbles about restlessly in its rocky bed. All that is pastoral stops. The solemn hush of the forest is irresistible: the characteristics of the flowers and birds have changed; the contrasts of light and shade are keenly dramatic" (41–42). Or later, when walking along the Long Island Sound at night in "Nature's Calm," she instructs the reader, "Step in the current; the black tide looks solid; you marvel the feet can move through it. Wade further in; up the water creeps as you advance. Swim! the cold and resistance seem to lessen as you cleave the liquid moonlight. It is a different world, yourself and Nature, yourself and space, with self a pigmy in it" (90).

In a sense, Wright's use of the second person represents the fundamental trope of her text, the "friendship" that lies at the heart of her philosophical interpretation of nature. Just as the second person point of view implies a relationship of interdependence between writer and reader, speaker and listener, so, too, does Wright's view of nature imply a fundamental connection between humans and the landscape. Though the figure of speech may seem quaint to contemporary readers, the "friendship of nature" could be seen as Wright's own attempt to describe the ecological relationship that has always existed between human beings and their natural environments. People cannot live without nature, Wright might argue, and nature cannot bring forth its bounty without the same kind of patient attention a gardener would give her garden. "If you serve Nature, waiting her moods, taking what she yields unforced, giving her a love devoid of greed, she will be a regal mistress," Wright notes in *Friendship*, "and all she has to bestow will be yours. Exact and say to one little field: 'This year you shall yield this crop or that,' and it becomes a battle-ground, where Nature, well equipped, wages war with man" (65).

Nature, in Wright's view, exists in relationship with human activity. Although people receive only peripheral treatment throughout most of *The Friendship of Nature*, Wright illustrates the interrelation between humanity and nature near the end of the text by interrupting her description of a picturesque winter landscape to refer to the smokestacks of Bridgeport, the "tall chimneys that breathe flame and cinders"—a moment reminiscent of the "complex pastoral" defined by Leo Marx in *Machine in the Garden* (1964). "Look at these chimneys also, though they break the harmonious circle, we must wear clothes and we must eat, for we may not all find sweetness in white oak acorns, like Thoreau. In winter, which lays bare the earth, man's needs appear, and intensify his personal limitations. Mutual dependence, and not isolation, was the plan of creation. Man needs the earth, and the earth needs man's stamp of progression" (134). Though the phrase "man's stamp of progression" may trouble modern ears, here Wright seems only to suggest that the pastoral landscape is an incomplete picture, that we cannot isolate nature from the products of human activity, cannot omit these smokestacks from the scene as Wright herself had once omitted them from her photographs.

As her statements in other publications illustrate, Wright was no advocate of unbridled industrial growth, but she was a realist who recognized that conservation cannot proceed apart from the communities that are its intended beneficiaries. In *Gray Lady and the Birds* (1907), for instance, she notes that the protection of birds is morally necessary "because we ourselves in our advancement are the main cause of their need of this protection, for as man increases, possesses, builds, and overflows the earth, so do these 'kindred of the wild' dwindle and silently disappear." Just as Wright chose to locate her bird sanctuary in close proximity to the Fairfield train depot, she argues in *The Friendship of Nature* that our understanding of nature must ultimately be local in character: sensitive to seasonal change, aware of regional variation, and grounded in scientific observation. As for her hope for the future of the conservation movement, we can consider the words she used to close her essay on "The Making of Birdcraft Sanctuary": "we have as yet only opened its gate to the beyond, and it is for us to make good in travelling a path in which the stepping-stones all take the form of question marks."

A New England May-Day

That it was May, thus dremede me.
—CHAUCER, *The Romaunt of the Rose*

Naturalized Narcissi at the Oaks

Do you know the tale of the months, the ancient Bohemian legend,—how by a fire which never goes out, sit twelve silent men each with a staff in his hand? The cloaks of three are white as snow, and three are green like the spring willow, and three are gold as the ripened grain, and three are blood-red like wine. The fire that never fails is the sun; the silent men are the months of the year. Each in his turn stirs the fire with his staff; for each has his office, and if one month should sleep and a turn be made amiss, then the snow would fall, bringing blight in spring, or drought would sere the harvest. This year April has overslept, and March has rudely jostled May, who in confusion takes up April's task, leaving its own for June.

Here in New England, we have no calendar of Nature, no rigid law of season, or of growth. The climate, a caprice, a wholly eerie thing, sets tradition at defiance and forces our poets to contradict each other. The flower which one declares the harbinger of spring may be a lazy vanguard in another year; the fringed gentian, set by Bryant in frayed and barren fields, frosty and solitary, usually follows the cardinal flower, in late September.

Come into the garden. The wind blows sharply from the north, where the snow still lies, and the clouds hang low, yet it is May-day, and a catbird is singing in the arbour. It is a much-trodden path in a long-discovered country, but each one discovers anew when he first sees it for himself. The golden touch, the guinea-stamp of Nature, is the dandelion in the grass border; flattened close to the sward, the wind passes over it, but bends and twists the masses of paler daffodils. The honeysuckles show pinched yellow leaves; the shrubs are bare, only the Forsythia is budded.

With what green intensity the pines are thrown into relief by the surrounding barrenness! In the top of one, a pair of crows are building, stealing forward and back with the distrust that is born of their small natures. Below, in a sheltered nook, patches of hardy violets are blooming: the little white violets that our grandmothers cherished, the odorous dark purple of the English garden-alleys, and the pansy-like variety from the Russian Steppes, which, as they bloom, laugh at our frosty weather. In spots where the sun has rested, the cowslip shows its budded panicles, and a friendly hedge shelters a mat of yellow primroses, the flower of Tory dames. The same hedge harbours each season innumerable birds. Hark! that broken prelude is from the veery, or Wilson's thrush, as he darts into his shelter. Where the stone wall gathers every ray of heat, are rows of hyacinths, with ponderous trusses of bloom, rivalling in variety and richness of colouring any bulbous growth, and hordes of bees are thumping about them. If you wish to study colour, then stay awhile by these pansies, that jostle and overrun the borders like a good-natured crowd of boys. It is strange that we rarely see the most beautiful varieties in the markets or the flower shows. The trade florists grow them more for size and less for jewel-like markings. Here are solid colours, hues, veinings, tracings, and varied casts of expression, harlequin, sober, coquettish, as if continual hybridization had placed human intelligence in them.

Not a leaf as yet on the hardy roses, and the sweet peas are only piercing the soil. The trellis skirting the garden is a lattice-work of wintry branches, but in the wren-boxes cleaning and building is advancing. Birds are not like flowers; the climate with them matters little; the food supply is the great question, and many a bird, sent south to winter by the ornithologists, will remain contentedly here, if grubs and berries are in plenty. The wren is, perhaps, the most capable bird of the garden, at once a cheerful, melodious singer, a thrifty provider, and a Board of Health in the care of its dwelling. Nothing that is dirty is allowed to remain about its snug quarters, and by a simple and comprehensive plan its local drainage is made perfect.

Go from the garden down through the lane to the meadow. What a burst of bird music greets you, solo, quartet, and chorus, led by the vivacious accentor, the golden-crowned thrush, with his crescendo of "Teacher—teacher—teacher!" This is the time and season to study the birds, while their plumage is fresh and typical, and they never sing so freely as in the first notes of their love song. The most puzzling part of the task is their modifications of plumage; for not only in many species are males and females totally different, but the male also changes his coat after the breeding season, and the nestlings wear a hybrid dress, half father, half mother. Does the gunner know that the bobolink, the jaunty Robert of Lincoln, whose glossy black coat, patched with white and buff, is so conspicuous in the lowlands when in May and June he rings out his delicious incoherent song, but who becomes silent in August and changed to a sober brown, is the reed-bird that he slaughters?

New songsters are arriving daily, some as birds of passage only, and others to remain. The bushes along the lane are alive with twittering guests. Now it is the wood-pewee, with his plaintive cry, or his brother the phœbe-bird, twisting and turning, who has built his nest under the porch for many a season, and out in the pasture the chipping sparrow is gleaning fibres and hairs for her nest. The spring of clear water in the dell is a great attraction to them; and as they bathe and drink, we can, with a field-glass, easily distinguish their markings. The robins have been building for a week, and high upon a hickory trunk a golden-winged woodpecker and a squirrel are contending loudly for a hole, which both claim for a nest. The sparrow tribe is appearing in force. That flock of brown and ash-coloured birds with white-striped crowns and white-patched throats are peabody birds, or white-throated sparrows; and if you look overhead, you will see that the charming little soprano is the song-sparrow. He is Nature's bugler who sounds a reveille from the March alders, and calls, "Lights out," to the smouldering autumn fires. Yesterday a flock of red-brown fox-sparrows, the largest of the family, were drinking at the spring, but to-day they have passed northward.

Look at the bank where the sun, peeping through, has touched the moss; there is saxifrage, and here are violet and white hepaticas, pushing through last year's leaves; lower down the wool-wrapped fronds of some large ferns are unfolding. The arbutus in the distant woods is on the wane, a fragrant memory. At the shady side of the spring are dog-tooth violets; and on the sunny side the watercourse is traced by clusters of marsh-marigolds, making a veritable golden trail. On a flat rock, almost hidden by layers of leaf mould, the polypody spreads its ferny carpet, and the little dicentra—or Dutchmen's breeches, as the children call it—huddles in clumps. The columbines are well budded, but Jack-in-the-pulpit has scarcely broken ground. On the top of the bank the dogwood stands unchanged, and the pinxter flower seems lifeless.

A brown bird, with reddish tail and buff, arrow-speckled breast, runs shyly through the underbrush, and perching on a low bush, begins a haunting, flute-like song. It is the hermit thrush. Its notes have been translated into syllables thus: "Oh speral, speral! Oh holy,

holy! Oh clear away, clear away; clear up, clear up!"—again and again he repeats and reiterates, until seeing us he slips into the bushes. Over the spring in the open is the thrush's kinsman, the brown thrasher, a large bird of muscular build, with specked breast and rust-brown back, who thrashes the air with his tail held erect. He is a mocking thrush, allied to the southern mocking-bird, and like him is a vociferous singer.

Beyond the meadow a heavy belt of maples marks the course of the river; the gray, misty hue of winter has gone from their tops and they are flushed with red; the willows are yellow, and here and there show signs of leaf, but the white birches loom grim and chilling, with their tassels only expanded, and the anatomy of tree, bush, and brier is as clearly defined as in January. Bluebirds are very rare this spring; some chipmunks invaded their house last year, an intrusion which they sorely resented; but a number of warblers are flitting about, and feeding on young twigs or bark insects. The warblers, though insignificant singers, have the most varied and beautiful plumage; for a week, a flock of the black-throated green species has haunted a group of hemlocks, lighting the dark branches with glints of their gold and green feathers. The swallows are skimming over the meadow, and yesterday a belted kingfisher sat high in a dead maple by the river, with a flock of jays screaming and quarrelling near him. The snowbirds, buntings, nuthatches, and kinglets have passed to the north, as well as most of the owl tribe; but the little screech-owl remains to blink in the summer woods. Yonder black cloud, settling on the great chestnut, is an army of purple grackles, our crow blackbirds, and their glossy kin with the scarlet shoulders, whose cry is a shrill "Quank-a-ree," is the red-winged swamp blackbird.

Far down the meadow, where the grass is coarse and sedgy, and dry tussocks offer a shelter, the meadow lark is weaving its nest, working so deftly that its home is practically safe from human invaders. See him there, striding along in the full splendour of his plumage, dark brown above, with speckled sides, wings barred transversely, with brown, yellow breast, black throat-crescent, and yellow legs; while his mate is hardly less brilliant.

We must turn homeward now, for the birds are hurrying to shelter, the wind is rising, and the sound of the waves on the bar, two miles distant, is growing distinct and rhythmic. Big drops of rain are rustling in the dry beech leaves, the smoke of burning brush has enveloped the spring and shut off the meadow. The logs blazing on the hearth will give us a cheery welcome, for the mercury in the porch registers only ten degrees above freezing. Is it November? No, surely, but one of the twelve months has slept, and so wrought all this strange contradiction. This is the first of the Moon of Leaves, the May-day of Old England, and we have gathered violets and daffodils, and we have heard the hermit thrush singing in the lane:—

> The word of the sun to the sky,
>   The word of the wind to the sea,
> The word of the moon to the night,
>   What may it be?

When Orchards Bloom

The robin and the bluebird piping loud,
Filled all the blossoming orchards with their glee;
The sparrows chirped as if they still were proud
Their race in Holy Writ should mentioned be.
—LONGFELLOW, *The Birds of Killingworth*

Hemlock Woods

A FTER a week of showers, the lightly veiled sun glows potent and compelling. The cloud drift blows from the west, the green meadow mist lifts, revealing a greener mist of tender leaves. An oriole, breaking into song, queries: "Will you? Will you really, really, truly?" and a meadow lark answers: "Spring o' the year; spring o' the year."

The woods and lanes are astir with the mysterious whispering of the opening buds; the grass has grown deep in the fields, and hides the fading violets, saying as it closes over them: "Sleep softly, I will protect you." Ceres, who has been a laggard for weeks, has suddenly awakened to her duty, as if Pomona, anxious for her harvest, had roughly shaken her. The garden is blazing with a flame of late tulips; bizarres, by-blooms, flakes, and parrots, with fringed and twisted petals. The primulas show many hues, from gold to deepest crimson with a yellow centre, and mingle their perfume with the various Narcissi, the double, whose blooms rival the Gardenia, the trumpet major, and the pheasant's eye,—the poet's Narcissus. Masses of lilies-of-the-valley are straggling into the full sunlight, in spite of the tradition which makes them hermits of the shade. Branches of amethyst lilacs hang over the gray stone wall, and as they sway to and fro, the bees, laden too deeply with honey, fall drowsily to the ground. Pear and cherry and plum blossomed together this year, and the ground is still powdered with a wealth of their corollas.

Look through the vista before you, over the fields and up the hillside, where the tree tops meet the sky; there are the blooming apple orchards, foam-white, or rosy as Aurora's fingertips. Flower, bird, man, what a triad these blossoming orchards typify; for man's dwellings are always near his orchards, and in the orchards are the birds. There they are free and confiding, as though they had the instinctive assurance that their greatest safety lies in the protective love of man, against man, and against the unpitying force of purely natural law. The hair-bird builds in the garden near the house; in your brier-rose, perhaps, that the vagrant cowbird may not lay an egg, unnoticed, in its nest. The catbird chooses a syringa bush by the walk, that he may chide and chat as you pass by. The robin takes for his abode the arbour, or the vine that wreathes the door; the sparrow tribe lie low upon the ground, in bush, or hedge, blending with earth, to cheat the sparrow hawk.

But if you would have the complete brotherhood of birds, come to the orchard. The old orchard, where the trees, long past their prime, are gnarled and bent and moss-grown toward the north, where different grafts on the same trunk are marked by different blooms, where vines conceal the walls, and the boughs are left untrimmed in thriftless beauty. The farm-house, standing only across the road, boasts of young, well-pruned trees, with white-washed trunks; but thrift, alas! is an iconoclast, and the most comfortably crooked boughs are cut away, and there are few worms to tempt bird appetites. Here in this ancient orchard there is no change, except the soft, renewing transmutation of decay. Year by year, the red-eyed vireo or his kin has hung a nest in the russet's forking branch, and called at the children who would boldly peer at it: "You will rue, you will rue, you will rue it." Yellow birds, gay in gamboge and black, who later hang like errant flowers on the thistle stalks, gather here to court and nest and plume the whole summer through, whistling like wild canaries. The king-bird of famed prowess, with crimson-streaked crest, doubles and darts in his keen pursuit of bees, and the yellow-billed cuckoo, with sturdy neck, cries gratingly, "Kuk, kuk, kuk," as he probes the caterpillar from the meshes of his retreat. The cedar bird, whose quaker coat is relieved by waxy red-tipped wings, builds his deep, soft-lined nest, thinking meanwhile of laden cherry trees; and in the tufts of grass out in the open, hovering above a nest that is merely a heap of twigs, the bobolink calls in a perfect ecstasy: "Bobolink o'wadolink, winterseeble-see me-see me-see!" The towhee hops among the bushes to lead you from his nest, flashing his wings and tail like Jenny Wren, and darting just above; his little prototype, the redstart, with breeze-ruffed feathers, seizes a tiny moth, and through the branches the bluebird's plaintive note drops liquidly. The yellow warblers, with cinnamon-streaked breasts, flutter in flocks, like autumn leaves, and in a branchless trunk, hollow and hoary, the white-breasted wood swallows colonize. Two catbirds spy an adder by the wall, stretched basking on the stones, and raising an angry cry, they hover and strike at it, and the adder, too numb from its winter sleep to comprehend and exercise its charm, drags itself into a hole. A woodchuck lifts its head above the grass and sniffs, then, half suspicious, it slinks flatly down the pathway to the brook and drinks with little conscious sips. Chipmunks and red squirrels scold and spring from branch to branch, seizing the blossoms to eat the succulent cores, and, if they can, to loot an unwatched nest. And over all the melody and fragrance, distinctly comes the droning fugue of bees, and, in a lower key, the cropping of the rich grass by eager cows,—a pledge of golden butter in the churn.

Follow the grass-grown road that lies between the garden and the farm. The orchard breath floats on before, goes with you, then straying, follows you, pervading everything; and, here and there, beside the very wheel-tracks, you find the orchard's offspring, the wild crab-apple tree, and the orchard birds become more shy and are wrapt in reverie, as if overshadowed by the mood of the wood birds.

Go to the wood, but with a lowered voice and a velvet tread, in sober, thrush-like garb, so that you may pass unnoticed. See how the blood is stirring in the winter-chilled shrubs by the path; the canes of the wild roses and briers are red, the bayberry bark is bluish gray, and the sallow an olive yellow. The shad-bush holds its feathers proudly above the weeds and brambles, though they are as fleeting as hoar frost in the morning. Under the fence the half-closed anemones nod and cluster; they are the wind flowers, for they bloom in a windy season. Jack-in-the-pulpit comes next; those growing in the shade are pale and slender, but in sunny spots they are vigorous and of a deep brown-purple, contrasting finely with the Solomon's seals, one hung with green bells, and the other, the false Solomon's seal, with a feathery terminal.

A gleam of white from the bank shows the white dogwood in its perfection, and mingling with it is the pinxter flower, clad in flawless rose. The brook breaks through, and bubbles under the road, and in the grass by the margin are winking bluets and white violets. Clinging to earthy stones and swaying about, now floating, now wholly submerged, is the pungent watercress, spreading its naked roots to keep its balance. Iris and arums are thrusting up their blades, near the heart-leaved pickerel weed and shining arrowhead. In compact bunches, rank and lusty, are the ferns that love wet ground, the various Osmundas, with their fronds of rusty spores.

Go further yet into the wood; the banks grow steep, the road winds through a glen to the side of a narrow river, which tumbles about restlessly in its rocky bed. All that is pastoral stops. The solemn hush of the forest is irresistible: the characteristics of the flowers and birds have changed; the contrasts of light and shade are keenly dramatic. Here are laurels, whose faithful leaves have braved the winter; the hop-hornbeam, poplar, oak, and hickory, chestnut, ash, beech, and towering hemlock trees. The ground-pine pierces the mould with its persistent antennæ-like stems, and the bellwort vibrates beside the useful wintergreen, which is not yet in flower. Over the river hangs a ruined mill, battered by ice and wind; and all about are worn millstones, some propping up the mill, and others crumbling away and overgrown by moss and ferns. Below it the river dashing through the gorge is spanned by a single rough-hewn tree, to bridge the way for children going through the woods to school; beyond the stream the hill ascends.

Not a bird note is heard, for topping a wind-scarred pine, a red hawk sits watching for prey. The undergrowth is scant, but mosses abound and blend with the veined leaves of the pipsissewa. Ferns hang their draperies on everything; frail zones of maidenhair, sensitive onoclea, the tufted Woodsia, the hay-scented Dicksonia, and feathered asplenium. Fissures in rock and bank still harbour little beasts,—the weasel, mink, skunk, raccoon, and even the fox, and a great horned owl, disturbed, swoops heavily and flies into deeper shade. The ground is spongy and the piney moss makes the foot slip, and the crushed petals of the purple trillium give out the odour of blood.

Under the hemlocks are scattered pairs of leaves,—broad, oval, rough, and ribbed lengthwise,—do you know their bloom? Look yonder, on a straight round stem is hung a pink-veined pouch, and above it, reaching up octopus-like, are greenish arms. It is a cypripedium, the Indian moccasin flower, beautiful as any orchid that the florist hoards. It was abundant here a little while ago, but like the Indian himself it shrinks from the civilizing touch, and when we meet them now, perched like a flock of tropic birds, we look our fill, touch and caress them, then come away, telling their refuge only to the bees.

Go backward to the road, by rocks iridescent with trickling moisture, whose crevices hold tufts of scarlet columbine. How science and a web of fancy identify our common flowers, and how undiscriminating ignorance jumbles and confuses them! Thus, honeysuckle may mean the columbine, clover, or the June vine on the porch; and red-bells stands, in local parlance, both for columbine and scarlet clematis. Turn to the names that science and legend give the columbine: Aquilegia, the Latin cognomen for a likeness of the flower's petals to an eagle's claws; Columbine, from the gaudy mate of Harlequin, for the resemblance of the flower to the cap which Folly wears; and another yet, touching both flower and season, handed down from the monks of old, who with loving sentiment wrought flowered margins to their missals and books of hours,—Columbine, a dove, the sign of the Holy Ghost, who descended in the cloven tongues of flame at the Feast of Pentecost; and so, to-day, at the Pentecostal season, the fiery tongues blooming on the gray New England rocks repeat the message.

The hawk has gone and the birds are singing once more, the water thrush, and the warbling vireo, and down the road the cattle saunter homeward from the pasture, and the orchard fragrance comes retrospectively, like a refrain that lingers in the memory.

Precious is the solitude and the song of the water thrush, for they soothe the spirit; precious are the orchards, the sunlight, and the home-going cattle, for they warm the heart. The red thrush perching high pours out his voluble song, while the lilacs sway over the wall. Still querying in an elm swings the oriole; is he bird, or flower, or cloud, or the transmigration of all?

The Romaunt of the Rose

I saw the sweetest flower wild Nature yields,
A fresh-blown musk-rose; 'twas the first that threw
Its sweets upon the summer.
    —KEATS, "To a Friend Who Sent Me Some Roses"

Madame Plantier Rose

THE twilight lingers, yearning for the rosy dawn. The breeze, laden with heavy odours, dissolves upon the earth in dew. The ox-eye daisy bends to the encircling grass, sighing: "He loves; he loves me not." From the hedge, the coral trumpets of the honeysuckle declare its sweetness, and the jewelled humming-bird pauses before it vibrant. The wood thrush ceases its song, and next the vesper-sparrow; one final ripple from the bobolink, a whistle from the chat, and then a veery, and the booming frogs alone disturb the silence. A night-hawk wheels, and low in the west the slender crescent moon yields precedence to Venus, the evening star.

In the still garden, from a bed of emerald leaves, slowly unfolding, perfume-clad, a queen comes forth, the first June rose. The brown moth, flitting, bears the news through the garden, fields, and lane. The fireflies signal it across the swamp, and perching in a tree, remotely sociable, his own breast flushed with joy, the grosbeak murmurs it all through the night.

The east at dawn is a barred fire-opal; before the prism changes, the herald tanagers, in red and black, are speeding through the trees, and in every field the tinkling bobolinks proclaim the climax of the sylvan year,—the birth of the first rose. Over all the land the rose-blood, pulsing in flower and fruit, claims relationship. The well-fed strawberry, with his ruddy, pitted face, calls himself cousin; the ripening cherry speaks for the plum, the pear, and the quince. The tall blackberry canes wave their snowy wands in homage, and in the springy fields, where the fleur-de-lis betray the sluggish stream, the avens shake their golden petals crying: "We too, we too are kin."

Then the gypsy clan, that camp in bush and grass and tree, ring out their matins, with the hair-bird as the leader; the mourning dove sings contralto, the hermit thrush, robin, song-sparrow, and bobolink are sopranos, the oriole and wood-thrush tenors, while cuckoos and highholes lend a croaking base. The catbird mimics and jeers in every key, and the green warbler adds his little prayer: "Oh, hear me! Hear me,

St. Theresa!" This is their pæan of joy, their perfect song, before the nesting cares ruffle their bright feathers, and scorching July suns weary and silence them.

With bird notes mingle the flower voices, in the language of quaint days, when flowers served as speech between shy lovers, and each young maiden working in her garden lived and dreamed in it. The flowering almond spoke of hope, the bluebell nodded constancy; the vigorous arum, ardour; the white poppy, closing with the early shadows, sleep; the pansy, thoughts; the larkspur, fickleness. But roses, whether they are red or white, pink-hearted or yellow, double or single, all sing of love, the changeful melody of many keys.

Young Cupid once, or so the legend runs, kissed a red rose, and in its heart put love. Alas! between its petals there lurked a bee that stung his lips. To still his cries of rage, his mother strung on his bow a swarm of bees, and plucking out the stings of others, set them upon the rose's stalk in punishment. So both love and roses are beset with thorns.

The wild rose, token of simple-hearted love, that stars the unmown edges of the fields and rocky banks, is the first of the wild tribe, coming before its paler swamp sister unfurls, or even the hardy little sand-rose bush has budded. The slender-stemmed musk-rose yields its fragrant charm only at evening; it is capricious love. The maiden-blush rose, well veiled in green, says: "If you love me you will find it out." The moss-bud answers: "I stand confessed." The banner rose, streaked with red and white, means war, in memory of the feuds of Lancaster and York, and the long-spiked Carolinian cries: "Dangerous is love." The sprayed white bridal rose says: "Happy love," and the sensuous damask, mother of Eastern altars, only echoes: "Love, I love." But the eglantine, the rose of sorrow, dropping its fragrant leaves like tears, whispers: "I wound to heal." Those who know only the winter florist's rose, the growth of forcing steam, do not know the poor man's rose, or the lover's rose, the free gifts of the sun, the air, and the dew, the marriage token of the earth to June.

Go into the garden now; do not delay! Roses are sweetest and keep longest when picked with the dew on them. Only yesterday the tulips were holding their cups brimming with light, and wallflowers mingled the sweetness of earth and sun. A few brief weeks ago, in the keen crisp air, we gathered primroses and violets. To-day the air is languorous, and the heat trembles above the gravelled path. Look at the beds of iris; some are royal purple edged with violet, others yellow laced with crimson, and in the corner, a group apart, are the white, with blue patrician veins and each stamen feathered with gold. See the spires of foxgloves, whose hairy, spotted throats allure the bumblebee, and the hardy poppy, who, borrowing Mephisto's name and cloak, burns in the bordering grass, next to masses of clove pinks, pure white and fringed. The tall blue larkspur, with flower stalks of mimic bees, completes the garden's tricolour, while the great peonies, red, crimson, and pink, might pose as roses for Gargantua.

Here are the roses, here and everywhere; they will almost leap into your arms. Fill your basket, your hat, your upturned gown, and still there will be enough to strew the ground with fragrance. They are not prim, set, standard trees, pruned like parasols, but honest bushes, hanging branch over branch, with clean leaves and lavish bloom. Ask General Jacqueminot for half-closed buds, his flowers flatten too soon in the open sun. Will you have darker? Here are Dr. Dombrain, Xavier Olibo, dressed in velvet, and Prince Camille Rohan, in crimson-black, and double to the heart. You may have pink ones too. No rose is half so much a rose as the great deep-cupped pink. Here is Paul Neyron, but he opens back too wide. Gloire de Margottin has a better shape, and Anne de Diesbach is a perfect globe. Will you have blush pink? Here are Captain Christy and the Silver Queen. Will you have buds? Here are pink and white moss-buds, and still another, without a single thorn, whose petals are the hue of some rosy, curled sea-shell. For pure white clusters we must beg of Madame Plantier, who vies in purity with the Coquette des Blanches. Pass by that Persian yellow; its saffron disks smell badly, and gather instead the eglantine, for its leaf is even sweeter than the flower.

Here by the trellised wall are nameless guests, the relics of more simple days when roses had no royal names, and cuttings from a neighbour's bush spread east and west. There are the cinnamon rose with brownish bark and dull-red spicy flowers, and the red rose of Provence, the rose of a hundred leaves, with hooking thorns, whose blossoms were much esteemed for rose cakes and conserves; and lastly the frail yellow brier with thorns like moss and flat, semi-double flowers.

In times when Gothic art followed in stone the teachings of the trees, the rose was wrought to be a window in the vast cathedral walls and called the rose of Heaven, whose vitreous petals symbolized blessèd souls.

Who is there but can conjure up tender memories with a rose?

Perhaps it may recall a wild rose hedge, smothered by elder flowers, where children came in recess time, to tie posies with the pliant grass and play at ring-a-rosy in the fields. Perhaps it may bring back a cottage home in a far-distant land, where the bees flew about the hives all day, and white jasmine strove with Gloire de Dijon roses in the thatch, and life was sweet,—until the mouths outgrew the bread, and parting came.

Perchance some old New England garden blooms again before the misty eyes. A giant elm shading the picket gate, the house yellow and white with olive blinds, and a pillared porch with narrow, high-backed seats, a honeysuckle training up one side to meet a prairie rose; a straight, flagged walk down to the gate, bordered on either side by myrtle and stiff zebra grass; with syringas by the side fence, a strawberry shrub and lilacs grown to trees. About the south porch were some tender plants in pots, an oleander and an orange tree in tubs; while drumming on the window-panes the golden laburnum swung, peeping in and out.

The great stone chimney had a hearty breath which needed no aid from chimney pots or tiles, and sheltered a tribe of swallows, who, poising high, dropped to their nests, then whirled aloft again like wind spirits. The well, with its long sweep, stood close to the back porch, a corner screened by hop and grape vines, where women sat and sewed of afternoons and talked with neighbours who stood leaning on the fence. Here the young people came from the garden with rose leaves in their aprons, and their mother took down the big blue jar, that "grandfather brought from China" and caged in it the sweets in fragrant potpourri, reading the rule, meanwhile, from her grandmother's book: "Take of June roses just about to fall, two parts. Shake them well free from dew, and add of new-blown buds two parts; of rosemary and lavender flowers and leaves take one part. Place in a jar with layer for layer of salt, and cover until the salt has drawn the juice (three days will do), then add some fresh rose leaves every day, and stir and mix them well. When you have filled the jar with well-steeped leaves, add ambergris, gum benzoin, allspice and cassia buds, a grain or two of musk, and four vanilla beans broken in bits. Of oil of jasmine, violet, and rose, add each an ounce to a full gallon jar."

A walk bordered with box led to the garden gate, half choked by woodbine, and once there, beauty and rude nature overran New England thrift. Johnny-jumpers peered between the stones; snowballs and weigela shrubs almost hid a fallen apple tree where indigo birds built their nests. Lupins and Londonpride, nasturtiums, touch-me-nots, grew side by side with fennel, thyme, and rue. Catnip and radishes, with tender lettuce-heads, were next to bouncing-Bet, sweet peas, and China pinks; and roses, pushing vigorous suckers out, walked freely all about the place and gathered thick around the moss-grown sun-dial.

Perhaps a recollection still more dear may rise. A gift of roses with the thorns picked off, a walk in summer ways but not alone, the choosing of a rose such as Lothair received from Corisande,—then bridal roses.

Oh, calm June days that overflow the night, and brief June nights that yield another day! oh, rose of June that by day and night breathes hopeful love! close in the starlit garden, far on the wood-dark hill, where the wind sweeps and the arching eglantine, raising its crown of thorns over lonely graves, whispers, "I wound to heal," and shares its vigil with the whip-poor-will.

The Gardens of the Sea

On the wide marsh the purple-blossomed grasses
Soak up the sunshine.

— LOWELL, "Summer Storm"

Wakeman's Island

THE sea was at war with the land long ago. The land stretched out an arm to bar its way, but the sea, chafed by the mute resistance, swept on across the beach, clove through the sand-crest where deeply rooted grasses bound the shifting particles, and spread upon the meadows, a salt rime, foaming and raging, until the tree-crowned knolls were islands, and the soil turned to stiff ebon ooze.

The sea-breeze met the land-breeze, and they roared to and fro above the marshy waste, disputing its possession. Upon their hill the Twelve Months sat in council to hear the tale of strife. December smoothed his frosty beard, leaned on his staff, and issued the decree: "These lands, henceforth, shall belong to no one. They shall be desired but yet debatable; yielding no crop but beauty, they shall be the gardens of the sea. Both land and sea shall blend their strength in their creation: the land-breeze sowing abroad a myriad seeds, the sea-breeze lending its fertile breath to quicken them. The sun and mist shall dye the coarse, rank grass with richest colours, and from the slime breed dragon-flies with painted wings, while birds of passage shall be sentinels and keep their watch throughout the year. If man shall till the marshes, then the sea will come, and lapping up his toil obliterate his steps."

The flush of morning comes upon the sea and pales the beacon's rays. The night mists shrink before the sun, and the low coast is revealed, a bar of copper. There is no breath of wind, not a ripple; the boats at anchor are motionless as sleeping swans. A fisherman, whose gray sail hangs idle above the piles of nets, poles his way up the creek, and the startled herons drop among the reeds.

On the land the trees, now in full summer leaf, bend low, and the drenching dews distil the scent of the mown fields. Between the sea and land lie the marshes; here and there men have essayed to build a dike to keep them from the sea, or pile a road to traverse them. Always the sea transcends their work, and pushing, swallowing, has kept its gardens to be a thing of dreams, a picture in twelve panels like the year.

Down from the village runs the dusty road; the plough uproots it, fall and spring, and turns the turfy edge and heaps it in a jolting crown. Following the plough, each autumn, careless men lop with their stubble scythes the wealth of flowers that make the waysides bright, and bare the shiftless fences.

The straight road lies past low cottages and onion fields; on either side of it the land is treeless; there are no birds but crows, that pry and sneak behind the mullein stalks, watching until some cottage woman comes to give her chickens corn. The road halts before a pair of bars, and with a sudden angle takes an inland turn, and at these bars the tillage stops, and all the other scars of toil. Stretching beyond, you see a cool, close lane, with lines of grass between the tracks of hoofs and wheel, and it invites, yes, quite compels, the tread of willing feet.

There are no fences here; where they were once a living barrier has sprung from their decay, and willows luxuriate. Tall sumach bushes follow up the line, then hickory saplings, silver birches, and choke-cherry trees, with here and there a group of sassafras or young maples, while wild grape vines bind the whole into a leafy wall, and freight the air with the fragrance of their blossoms. Meadow-rue sends up its foamy-tipped stalks above the pink milkweed whose globes are food for butterflies, and glowing wild roses, crimson more than pink, from the deep, strong soil, powder the blundering bumblebees with gold pollen. On every side, broad cymes of white elder flowers reflect the light, and rough-fronded brakes line the path.

The upland fields of timothy that border on the lane are not yet mown, and field sparrows warble and swing on the stout grasses. Yonder in that briery maze a yellow-breasted chat is hiding, who calls with a ventriloquist's whistle, until a dozen birds seem answering. The madcap bobolinks are now anxious to disperse their broods before the mowers lay bare their shabby nests; and half bewitched, they sing, and pausing, float with outspread wings, then soaring, pour out torrents of high notes,—*allegro-con fuoco*.

In the black alders further down the lane sound notes of warning. Circling above the trees, a red-winged blackbird, trig as an hussar, is uttering cries in a shrill falsetto voice, while his rusty mate flits in and out in agitation. Pull back the bushes and you will find their nest, hanging upon a stalk by twisted strands of sedge, and in its deep, soft bowl are cradled two light blue eggs with umber spots, and two young birds. But now the frantic parents have aroused all their kin, and twenty birds or more are on the wing, screaming at once.

Look through the button bushes with their feathered balls, here on the seaward side. There lie the marshes, and the lane slopes down and bounds them until it melts into the green morass, and all the rest is trackless. What do you see? A cloth of soft warm green stretched toward the sea, a silver thread of water, fold by fold, embroiders it, framing with curious patterns the still, mirror pools. Long bands of dark oak woods lie on either side; before you are some tufts of sand grass, and a few dwarf trees are outlined black against the sky, while beyond the crest the boats slip through the golden haze. No colour of the spectrum but you will find it there at some time in the rounded year. Dominant now are purples, browns, and yellows merging into greens that stain the ground, until the sea and sky, meeting, absorb them.

Thread through this pathless garden, now stepping on grass hummocks to leave the sucking mud, now going dry-shod over drifted sand heaps and through belts of brakes, struggling waist-deep among the clinging fronds, but watching for the treacherous ditches where bending reeds join hands over the little tide channels, and the cat-tail flag, with its flat green leaves, holds up its rusty mace, and grasses that twist about the feet, ensnaring you, conceal the oozy ground.

At the first step the bindweed holding the grass by its spiral curves arrests you, and lifts its rosy chalice. Beyond are a bristling regiment of yellow thistles with bayonets fixed, and between them, flat on the soil, the star grass shines. The great blue flag still lingers, though long out of season, beside wide mats of sundrops, the diurnal mate of the paler evening primrose.

The ferns and brakes that border the low woods thin into groups and mingle with the swamp rose and blueberry. A streak of lovely mauve on a closer view reveals masses of calopogon, a flower of the orchid's tribe, clustered on slender stems; its hinging lips are bearded with hairs, yellow, white, and purple, while near by, where the grass is shorter, blooms the fragrant rose pogonia, both fringed and crested, also an orchid. Over all the flowers and grasses, the swallows skirt and dip, and high above some vagrant clouds cast dazzling shadows, and the breeze, full of sea-moisture, leaves salt upon the lips. This is today, but yesterday the beauty was as great; last month the soft new greens were brighter still, and as the year wears on the colours burn and deepen, and the herbage grows richer and more luxuriant.

In winter, when the frost-crust hid the ground and the caked ice banked the stiffened creek, the reeds and sedges, long since gone to seed, rustled and cracked in the wind, etching clear shadows on the snow. The stripped bushes, with every twig articulated by crystal points, were perches for the owls, and on the wooded knoll, by the creek's mouth, the eagle watched high in a tattered oak. The starving crows winged past like silhouettes, and the gulls, with hollow laugh, swept morsels from the sea, and at sunset all the scene was suffused with a cold purple glow.

Next came the vernal equinox with its swelling tides, which over-leaped the shore and swept away the barriers that the frost had set. The south creek and the east joined hands in amity, and made the marshes one vast, surging lake. The welcome osprey brought promise of good things:—

> She brings us fish, she brings us spring,
> Good times, fair weather, warmth, and plenty,

and, gathering the flotage of sticks and seaweed from the shore, built a wide-spreading nest in the same tree where in winter the eagle perched. Then, as the waters fell, the herons came, the red-breasted sandpiper, golden plover, and the snipe. The green bittern also, who stayed, and for food quarried from the mud the larvæ of the dragon-fly. The long-stemmed marsh violets pushed above the upland grass; on the sand ridges bloomed white sprays of beach plum, and the bayberry put out its pungent leaves.

The spring slipped on to summer, and land birds filled all the bushes with colour, life, and song; the trees concealed their limbs with pliant draperies, and the sea-gardens bloomed again and glowed with flowers. The sky at evening wore cool reflections of the west, at morn-ing bathed in mist, and all day long shaped fancies of its own; catching lights and burying them in the sea; piling angry fortresses only to riddle them with thunderbolts and cast them down upon the dunes in showers, holding a rainbow in their stead. The black waters of the creek double in its depths the shifting scenery, the storm clouds and the lightning forking down, the rainbow resting upon the leaden sea, the full moon, the sailing hawk, and the winking stars. As July length-ens, the spraying bloom of the sea-lavender spreads over the salt grass; and where fresh springs mingle with the bog the sundew, with its honeyed, fly-ensnaring leaves, buds out beside the pitcher plant, in whose water-laden carafes unwary insects drown themselves. On the dunes the prickly Indian fig expands its yellow wheels, pressing the sand closely in its love of heat. A band of flame edges a mass of reeds, and the deep-rooted Philadelphia lily, orange-red, lifts its spotted cups, and straggling toward the lane in dryer soil, the Canada lily hangs its whorls of red or yellow bells, like miniature pagodas.

In August a wave of orange-yellow covers the ground. On stiff leafy stalks, the yellow-fringed orchid blooms in short, densely clustered spikes. Its rare beauty and tropic colouring attract the fertilizing bees, and allure the girls who revel in the air and sun to search for it in the sea-gardens. Under the hickory shade on the dry knoll you will find the oak-leaved yellow Gerardia, a shy recluse, with half-exotic flowers, that hold their rank with garden pentstemons and tender gloxinias. In August, too, a ruddy glow spreads on the marshes when the great rose-mallow blooms and trails its sheets of pink all up and down, wading deep in ditches with the flowering rush, following the lanes and zigzagging across the meadows; and in its wake trudge the sunflowers with their golden coronets. The clethra bushes in the deep runnel on either side of the lane, pluming with spicy bloom, are latticed in and out with white wreaths of clematis. The sea-pink, spreading its carpet, repeats the mallow's colour, and the frail maritime Gerardia echoes it still further.

The falling tide has left bare the edges of the creek, and in a slouching boat the crabber feels his way between the shoals, his net held low and his eyes fixed on the sidling shadows underneath. On the marsh-islands mowers gather up the rough, salt hay and pile it on flat barges, and, with the rising tide, float slowly inland on the water road, like some strange hybrid wains, akin to those that glide dikewise between the Holland fields, piled high with flowers and produce from the farm, with dun-brown sails for horses.

The keen September winds kindle the autumn fires, and reds, yellows, and purples hold their final tournament. The stubbly meadows wear a yellow tinge, which blends to brown in the shorn marshes, while the goldenrod has filled the place of wild rose, orchid, and mallow. Wands of the blazing-star, and the various asters, purple the fields and lane, where the pokeberry with crimson stem and fruit vies with glazed sumach leaves. Virginia creeper wraps the tallest trees in scarlet, and up and down, wasting the beauty of the marshes and the lane, the fire goes and creeps with briers through the scorched brown grass. Maples and sumach, sassafras and oak, burn slowly out, leaving the clematis smoking, while a dull yellow flame consumes the brakes and weeds.

Then the wild ducks gather, and before the autumn storms, the plover, flying low, falls a prey to gunners hidden in the reeds, and the brown moulted bobolinks, no longer songbirds, are shot ruthlessly. The east winds come and bring wild tides that beat and pile the seaweed on the sand, and long rains veil the marshes. The sharp-prowed duck-boat pierces through the flags in the gray of the late dawn, and tired geese pause in their flight to rest. The shortened days are broken by swift sunsets, the nights are steel-blue and touched by electric fingers pointing from the north. Frost flowers bloom and gem the heaps of leaves, and men come out and cut the sedge grass, the last yield of the marshes. Beauty still lingers and the sea is murmuring of its gardens, and with its siren voices greets the returning gulls.

Gliding through the night, torch in hand, his eel spear poised, the boatman calls, then listens. Answering from upper air are whirling wings, and birds of passage troop like untiring sentinels.

A Song of Summer

Shine! shine! shine!
Pour down your warmth, great sun!
While we bask, we two together.
—Whitman, "Out of the Cradle Endlessly Rocking"

English Larkspur, Seven Feet High

THE south wind sweeps over the mignonette, passing through the hedged sweet peas into the wood gap. The reeds on the brink of the river tremble and the pendulous red-gold meadow lilies ring the midsummer in with their clamouring bronze tongues. It is not the sungod's day of the Julian calendar, the summer solstice; not the festival of St. John the Baptist, when old English custom trimmed the doors with St. Johnswort and green branches, when a wheel bound with straw was taken to some neighbouring hill and set on fire and then rolled down to bear away harm and mark the sun's descent; but middle July, the New England midsummer, the half-way stile between the first cautious growth of June and September's ripening.

A haze drops between the sky and the earth, laden with oppressive heat; the deeply shadowed porch is airless, and under it the two dogs lie panting and exhausted. Ben-Uncas, a St. Bernard, who loves cold and snow, dreams of the river, and Colin, a veteran setter, thinks of the fern copse where the rabbits hide.

We two stand together out in the full sunshine, with the summer surrounding us, pulsing in the hot earth under our feet, and with summer in the heart. Spring is a restless season, the time of mating, planting, hoping. The sap flows into dry branches and the river leaps along madly, but summer, with its poppy-fringed cloak, brings the peace of fulfilment.

Standing in the sunlight, we listen and hesitate; the wind whispers as it passes and brings alluring messages. The trees call us to come to their shade and learn the birds' secrets, to rest on their moss-cushioned trunks, and listen to the music of the brook as it makes harp-strings of their pushing roots and sings the Song of Summer. So, persuaded, we go out through the midsummer ways, and the dogs reconnoitre before us as scouts.

The weeds and flowers are mingled together along the roadside, and the loiterer treasures many things that the farmer casts out of his fields. The yellow-starred St. Johnswort traces the path, and the grimy burdock, meshed with dust-hung cobwebs, crowds the moth-mullein, and wild carrots spread their filmy umbels beside brown stalks of last year's dock. Creeping, with clean, green leaves, the yellow hop-clover spreads and mats with the sweet white clover escaped from the fields. The yellow toad-flax, or butter and eggs, a cousin of the garden snapdragon, with its densely packed racemes, steps in and out, climbing on stone heaps, tangled thick with trailing blackberry vines, underneath whose leaves lies the ripe, sweet, astringent fruit. Tasting it, we suck the purple drops of summer wine, and drinking, grow in tune with Nature's melodies.

A silvery warble and the ripening thistles show a hovering flock of yellow birds, braving the prickly stalks for the sake of the winged seeds and down, to line their nests. For this gay bird builds late, though he has been here a long time; he waits for the ripening of certain seeds to feed his young. "Ker, cher, chè, chè! just look at me!" he calls, and straightway roughs his golden breast and fanwise smooths out his sable wings, speeding with a dipping flight to his shy olive mate, whistling softly, "We two, we two."

On each side of the road stretch the rough stone walls, skirting the pastures, intersecting fields and overgrown wood lots. The chipmunk darts in through the chinks, and gambols, whisks up a branch that holds a nest and hides again from the angry birds. The fields of straight-limbed timothy have cast their seed, and already we hear the clattering buzz of the horse-mower. Toppling, the grass falls sideways into lines, and much labour is saved, even though the scythe circled with a truer rhythm.

On the hillside they are cradling rye. The long awned heads sway on the glistening stalks, the breeze ripples this golden sea, and billowing it, a wave of music passes across, as if Pan was blowing softly through his oaten pipe a gentle prelude to the jovial harvest dance. Behind the cradle lies the prostrate rye, screening the sharp stubble, and here and there the pink-purple corn-cockle blends its flowers with the gold. In the neighbouring trees and bushes the birds lurk, waiting for the noontime silence, that they may gather up the gleanings.

Back of the rye field, a round knoll is topped by blooming chestnut trees. All the light and fragrance of the day is meshed by their feathery stamened spikes, and sifting through the mass of restless leaves, it refracts and breaks in countless tints. Romping all down the hill like jolly Indian babes, are troops of black-eyed-Susans, gay in warm yellow gowns. Perched on the road bank, nod blue campanulas, one of a tribe of half-wild things that escaped from gardens to beautify the roads and fields; only they strayed away so many years ago, that they seem completely merged in their surroundings and quite to the manor born.

An herby odour rises from the path, and in a space of less than twenty steps, sweet mint, catnip, wild thyme, yarrow, camomile, and tansy yield a bunch of simples, such as once hung on the rafters of every country garret, ready to be brewed in teas for various aches and pains. History, even in science, still repeats itself, and the peppermint, steeped into the tea that Lydia Languish might have sipped for the vapours, is now distilled and ministers to the nerves under the name of menthol, and the leaves of winter-green, that gran'ther chewed for his rheumatics, still pursue the same complaint, wearing its Latin name, Gaultheria. But do not let us talk of ills and medicines in mellowing summer-time, when the sunshine draws stagnation from the blood and clears its channels. To-day let the world slip, and let us live in a summer reverie.

The locust drowses in the open places and the shade stops as we pass a strip of onion fields. The deep, flat soil is cleared of every tree or bush that might give shade or take the substance from it. Outside the fence, some great elms lie rotting, elms that were hewn down because they barred the eastern light, and sent out too many thirsty roots to suck the richness of the field. The useless onion stones, gleaned from the much-tilled ground, are piled between the trunks of the decaying trees, and nettles and wormwood sprout vigorously about them.

If you serve Nature, waiting her moods, taking what she yields unforced, giving her a love devoid of greed, she will be a regal mistress, and all she has to bestow will be yours. Exact and say to one little field: "This year you shall yield this crop or that," and it becomes a battleground, where Nature, well equipped, wages war with man.

The bare onion field is the last stand of all. In early springtime, all the ground is smoothed and swept of every pebble, and the seed is sown. If it is not rotted by too copious rains the toil begins as soon as the lines of misty green appear. In the morning, when the malarial breath steams from the soil, rank with dung, the ragged boys crawl silently astride the rows, plucking the weeds, and women too sometimes, shapeless and pitiful to see. Prostrate and crouched, the slow procession kneels, as if in supplication to the sun to yield a crop, who, heedless, blisters and scorches them, as day by day they creep before his force, eyeing the ground like the Trappist monks, who each day claw the mould out with their fingers, digging their own graves. No flower cools the eye, no bird note thrills the senses, the very crows desert the onion field, and the dogs, with lolling tongues, slink beside the wall. O truth painter of Barbizon, this, this is Toil! You gave your earth-worn peasants the vesper bells to round their day,—the factory whistle is the New World's Angelus.

The dogs are true philosophers. While we, absorbed, still look over the quivering field, heat-sickened, they go on before, and spying a wayside pool, scatter the prim, important geese, and rolling in the shallow water, drink and bathe at once. Again we welcome the trees; thick maples arch the road, turning up the silver lining of their leaves in every whiff of air. Yonder is the bank of elecampane and the old locusts, and here are the mossy bars that lead to welcome depths of shade. Ben bounds over, shaking his wet coat, and rolls headlong in the deep, wild grass beyond; the path goes to the river and he knows it very well, knows every deep cold spring and muskrat run, knows also that all day he may run wild, and in an ecstasy he leaps and dashes to and fro.

Colin once followed the track of every field-mouse, scented the birds when neither human eye nor ear could detect them, crossed the country straight, leaped ditches, swam streams, but now grown old he waits until the bars are dropped, pretends he does not scent the trails he may no longer explore, and trusting us to choose an easy way, follows, looking up and rubbing his soft ears against us, his great brown eyes mutely confident; turning to man, to his dog-brain a god, to spare his age. Now wading deep in a maze of grass, weeds, ferns, we press through the unkempt lot to a great band of trees, and from them toward the heated body comes a wave of coolness, grateful as a refreshing draught to the lips or as music to the heart.

Small pointed cedars and young oaks mix with the undergrowth, and the tall staghorn-sumach, broken away to make a path, hedges it, offering delicious greens to our bouquet,—the dull green, red-stemmed leaves and the lighter panicled flowers, the whole blending with slender vines of the frost grape. The ground becomes moister, tall lady-ferns and cinnamon Osmundas wave with the heavy sway of palms, and a perfume unlike wood-odours, dense, tropical, suggestive of Gardenias or bridal stephanotis, steals on the questioning sense. A few steps further and a mass of white conceals the bushes, and we find the swamp-azalea, called viscosa, from the viscid honey of the flower. In runnels by the roadside you may often meet this bush, broken by cattle or by the careless passer, with the blossoms browned by heat; but here in the rich muck, screened from the fierce noon sun, it grows unscathed and opens flower by flower in all perfection.

An upward pitch rolls to the crest of woods, and smaller ferns make the undergrowth; overhead are oaks and beeches; here and there a silver birch gleams with light, and from a copse of dogwood, cornel, pepperidge, black thorn, some aspens twirl and balance their odd leaves as if trembling with excitement. Entering the woods on a full summer day, it always seems as if another world of thought, speech, and sense lay open, that the mystic wood-sounds, the creaking of interlacing branches, the snapping of twigs, and leaf lappings, might be construed as a language to tell of the tree's life and desires. For trees are totally unlike in their moods and influence, and give out their individual impress of joy or gloom, strength or variability, each according to his character. No one would tie chaplets of willow for a conqueror, or weave garlands of oak leaves for a bride. Stones washed from the banks by the winter storms are frescoed by lichens, and between them are tufts of ebony spleenwort; swinging by drooping branches, we reach the summit, and resting on the deep, soft moss, look on, through the sun-flecked tree boles, to a trackless wilderness of wood and leafage, unscarred as yet by the axe, unspoiled by man's touch. A giant chestnut crowns the place, with a four-branched trunk, as if some well-filled burr had seeded where it fell; while underneath it is one unbroken stretch of moss.

Summer is singing its noon song, and we listen, leaning against the tree, as if, sibyl-like, it might whisper to us. Trees surge and the sun sifts through with sapphire sky glints; the spider-webs are idle, Arachne is napping. A black and white lizard comes into a sunny spot, and a locust, splitting the back of his pupa, crawls out on a root, his wings yet limp and moist from the mysterious change of condition. The golden-crowned thrush wakes fitful echoes in the trees by the river; the wood thrush tunes and then lapses to silence. The leaf-shadows dance, the branches above us make strange hypnotic passes, and the heat-veil is stealing over the pastures:—

Woof of the fen, ethereal gauze,
Woven of Nature's richest stuffs,
Visible heat, air-water and dry sea,
Last conquest of the eye;
Toil of the day displayed, sun-dust,
Aerial surf upon the shores of earth,
Ethereal estuary, frith of light,
Breakers of air, billows of heat,
Fine summer spray on inland seas;
Bird of the sun, transparent winged,
Owlet of noon, soft pinioned,
From health or stubble rising without song,
Establish thy serenity o'er the fields.

—THOREAU

And the old tree murmurs: "Rest is the summer song of noonday."

The breeze revives, and the shadows, drawn in by noontide, drop to eastward; a fragrance wafts from the moss tufts and guides us to its giver,—the dainty pipsissewa,—growing in bunches and masses, sprouting from creeping rootstalks, with a stem of madder-lined dark leaves with creamy veinings, crowned by waxy white flowers, their petals reflexed, having flesh-coloured stamens and a willow-green centre. This is the last of the spring tinted and scented flowers that carpet the woods, thriving in its shadows. Who can describe its perfume? It is a combination of all the wild, spicy wood-essences, refined and distilled by the various chemical changes from the autumn-dyed leaves to their mould, that rears the flower in its bosom. From a heap of slowly crumbling brown leaves, the Indian pipe protrudes its ice-white, scentless flowers, that blacken at the gentlest touch, and though of the pipsissewa's clan, they are a parasitic growth.

The old setter stretches and yawns, but his companion is always fresh and ecstatic, and bounds down the slope to the river, trampling through the sweet-fern bushes, snapping dead branches, heedless of briers, and leaving a path where we may follow. Coiled on a stump, sunning himself, but not at all sleepy, lies a flat-headed adder, of a brownish colour, patched with a darker brown, and with the upper lip horny and aggressive. Instantly there springs up the old grudge born in the Garden of Eden, but Eve cautiously holds aloof, fearing perhaps that she may be further tempted, and Adam, replacing the Biblical heel with a stone, promptly bruises the serpent's head. Whether they are hurtful or not, snakes always seem a token of evil, the sign of some sinister power, and doubly so when we come upon them amid birds and flowers.

Again the undergrowth changes, and grows bolder. Great bushes of meadow-sweet appear,—the wild white spirea salicifolia,—burr-reeds, and flowering sedge, with thickets of spurred jewelweed, and feathers of the late meadow-rue. Parting the tall weeds, we pushed through, and the odour of peppermint, crushed by our tread, rises about us; butterflies hover in flocks above the purple milkweeds, and the river glistens between the sallows. It is not a great stream carrying a burden of traffic, but a sociable, gossiping sort of a river, bearing the small tattle of mill-wheels, hidden in byways and corners, bringing down some bark from the saw-mill, or a little meal-foam from the grist-mill; scolding the pebbles, but growing silent as it passes the pools where the pickerel, like motionless shadows, hide under projections. In a bit of curled bark, drifted into a shallow, a song-sparrow bathes, and chirps an answer to the babbling water. If he would, he might tell us the story of the river. We sit on the bank and watch as he preens and spatters and flies to a brier, warbling with a heaving breast, his heart-beats keeping the rhythm, until the meaning of the river is blended in his song. Ben half wades, half swims in the water; Colin renews his youth at the fresh draught he laps, while down the river races to the willows:—

Sing willow, willow, willow.

Is there any other tree that sings the river's measure so truly? The name itself is music, and its pendulous branches sweep an accompaniment to the melody of the water.

All through the afternoon we follow the river bank; the stream divides, and branching, trails its beauty through an open field, but the deeper channel still keeps to the woods and meets the straggler in the mill-pond. The pond's edge is thickly hedged and the bushes are tied together by wiry dodder; the heart-leaved pickerel-weed, with its purple spikes, outlines the shallow water, and the lily pads, whose flowers are closed or closing, rock with the gentle motion.

A kingfisher perching in a sycamore, above the mill house, dives suddenly; his reflection is so distinct that he seems to wrestle with himself under the water. One by one the birds begin to warble as the sun slants behind the cedars that top the hill, and we sit in the enclosing shadows. The colours of the submerged clouds circle and eddy with all the shifting hues of a bubble, and blend in an endless prism. The dogs, unnoticed, have slipped away and gone home. The shadows lengthen and then cease, passing to dark reflections; a mistlike breath comes from the water. A night-hawk, with white-spotted wings, skirls high in the air, and others answer. We two wait with full hearts. Silent in the present content, as in an endless vista where the past and future meet in the present.

A star flowers out, then another, heat lightning quivers at the horizon, a bat flaps low, the wind drops through the willows, and the pond grows black and glassy as we listen for the song of evening. From the clouds to the water the words come like an echo:—

Rest is the even-song of summer.

Feathered Philosophers

You cannot with a scalpel find
    The poet's soul, or yet the wild bird's song.
        —*A Wood Song*

The Dell at Mosswood

M AN'S kingdom is a bit of ground and his birthright a resting-place on the earth's bosom. Out of the ground grow the trees that hang their leaves in the wind to shelter him, the flowers that unfold in the sun, the ferns that deepen the silence in the shadowy byways where the lichens trace their cryptograms on the rocks. Above this bit of ground is a scrap of sky holding its rotary star treasure, showing the season's various signs, and on the ground, in the trees, and in the sky, are the birds; through the heat, and in the cold, sociable or remote, one for each thought, one for each mood, one for every passion. A bird for every day, from the ghostly white owl skimming the January meadows, to the humming-bird that darts roseward in the midsummer twilight.

The sun in its journey from equinox to equinox marks out the seasons, but they are brought nearer to the eye and heart by the shifting calendar of feathers that measures the seasons by its songs, changes of colour, and comings and goings. The birds are more time-true than the flowers, who may be hidden by late snows, or cut off by early frosts. To claim the confidence of one feathered brother, to compass his ways and learn his secrets, to fathom his traits and philosophy, to gain recognition from him, is a labour worthy of trial.

The character study of the bird is beyond the mazes of classification, beyond the counting of bones, out of the reach of the scalpel and the literature of the microscope. We comprehend its air-filled bones, and its physical evolution, uses, and limitations. We know that it is frailly mortal,—but still a bird will seem like a voice from some unknown region. The beasts of the earth are bound to its face, and man also, for science, as yet, can guide but very poorly even the most limited aerial navigation; but the bird appears, in a way, to surmount the attraction of gravitation, and, as its eulogist Michelet says, "feels itself strong beyond the limits of its action."

Instinct may serve to designate such acts as the sex impulse or that bear the stamp of heredity, but a wider scope must be allowed to the brain of the bird, which with keen sense and a trite philosophy often outshines in manners and morals some of the human animals.

Have birds a language? Surely they have between themselves a spoken understanding, which the least discerning man may translate, and distinguish between their cries of joy and of fear; may separate their love songs and their scolding from the subtle ventriloquism that lures the searcher from a nest. The chronicler of the Val Sainte Veronique says that a superstition still lingers there,—the belief that every bird repeats some phrase of its own, and that in every village there is some one who understands and could interpret it, but that he is in honour bound to guard the knowledge until when on his death-bed; then he may reveal it to his nearest of kin; at such a time, however, his thoughts being upon other things, the secret is lost.

It is more likely that in the sleep which precedes birth, the forces of Nature stamp impressions upon the white brain-mass and string the latent senses to keen susceptibility, which later, in their full development, vibrate at Nature's lightest touch. So from prenatal circumstance some beings are more closely drawn toward the creatures of air and earth and comprehend their voices:—

> We are what suns and winds and waters make us;
> The mountains are our sponsors, and the rills
> Fashion and win their nursling with their smiles.
>
> —LANDOR

People who care little for birds because of their lovable qualities, or for their ministry to eye and ear, still associate them with signs, warnings, and supernatural power. In an old legend, Death is pictured going through the land with a bird perched upon his shoulder and choosing his victims by its aid. The bird tapped at a window, and if, through heedlessness or fear, the casement remained closed and shelter was refused it, Death knocked the same night. If the bird was admitted, Death passed on.

> "Knock at this window," said Death.
> In flew the bird, scant of breath:
> They fed him, succoured him, let him fly.
> Death passed by.

And even now people shiver when a wind-driven bird dashes against the pane, and half-smiling, fear, as they do when a mirror quivers and breaks. The negress also, a victim of voodoo, with rolling eyes and bated breath tells stories of the magic Zombi bird, which if it is killed and eaten continues to sing inside its murderer, revealing the sin of which he has been guilty.

What is more human in its expression than the despair shown by a caged wild bird? Its first mad impotent struggles, the head turned back as it searches in vain for a loophole of escape, and then the silent drooping attitude of heart-broken anguish. Such things always move me to a pitying vengeance. "I can't get out, no, I can't get out," wailed the starling, when Sterne tore vainly at the wires of its cage, and he wrote: "I never had my affections more tenderly awakened."

By accident, I once had two wild birds that showed a human likeness in the different ways with which they bore imprisonment. One bitterly cold Christmas eve, I bought them from a street pedlar, my only wish being to take them in from the numbing cold, and in spring to let them fly away. One was an English goldfinch and the other a siskin. Each had a cage with water and food, placed in a subdued light, to calm its strugglings more easily. The siskin was of a Byronic mood, fought against comfort, twisted the cage wires, would neither eat nor drink, and in the morning I found him hanging dead with his head between the bars. The goldfinch, when I brought him home, let me hold his draggled body in my hands, until their warmth had unbent his stiffened claws, so they might grasp the perch; then he shook himself, took a sip of water and a seed or two, and fell to smoothing out his wings and coat, pluming slowly. If a feather hung besmeared and broken he bravely pulled it out, and, his self-respect restored, he settled comfortably for the night, head under wing.

Never afterward did he show any signs of fear, but when I whistled to him he would always come close to the cage bars and make a soft kissing sound and part his beak. When springtime came, I found that to let him fly meant solitude and perhaps starvation. One mild day, I hung his cage in a low tree, when suddenly a tremor shook him, and throwing back his head he looked up through the leaves where the insects buzzed, as if the remembrance of some forgotten time had come back to him, and beating his wings, he fell from the perch with his eyes closed; but when taken indoors he rallied quickly, and lived, singing and cheerful, for many years.

The sky was gray, unrevealing, dumb; the earth was covered with ice crystals; the snow dropped its obliterating veil between the two, and there was no sun to mark the season by its position. Was it midwinter? No one could tell by mere sense of vision. Colin lifted his head, and extending his moist, vibrating nostrils, sniffed suspiciously. The black-capped titmice, the brown and white buntings, and the slate-coloured juncos fearlessly picked up the crumbs near his kennel, and the nut-hatch, less trustful, seizing a morsel, took it to a more quiet place. Colin, raising himself, crept softly toward the copse of spruces, lifting his feet from the new snow with cat-like deliberation. Did he hear the crossbill snapping the scales from the pine cones? Hardly that, for the flock, seeing him, had changed their position, and he halted before the spruces with his paw raised and tail rigid. Was it midwinter? Ah! the dog had found augurs to answer that question. Perched in the spruces were a score of sturdy male robins, not the gaunt resident birds who had fasted and battled with the rigours of winter, but the plump scouts of the coming spring, with the alert, well-fed air of migrants. The gray sky and white earth may cling to the winter curtain, but the bird heart beating warm leads us to March in the calendar; and when the snow-cloud divided, I could see that the sun was hurrying toward the vernal equinox, and I knew that the snow buntings would soon hasten northward after the white owls.

Again the sky was gray and the woods were choked and matted with brown leaves, the storm-stirred brook was brown, and the grass also. Was it dead autumn or unawakened spring? There stole into the sky a rift of blue, and on the ground lay the azure feather of a bluebird's wing, his spring sign this, for his autumn coat is rusty. The dun sky swallowed up the blue again, and near the bluebird's feather lay a hawk's barred quill. Comedy and tragedy side by side. Which overcame? the hawk by force, or the bluebird by escape,—who knows? But in a neighbouring farm-yard above a hen-coop swung a dead hawk, compelled by the wind to flap his wings in warning.

In early April two robins came to the leafless vine on the western piazza and began a nest. In the morning snow fell, and in the evening lightning blazed. The birds were discouraged, but after a few days returned and completed their dwelling, and another pair chose a trellis over the foot-path, and still another an evergreen branch by the road-side. All three nests were in plain sight, and I watched their comings and goings at intervals from morning until evening. The father and mother alternately covered the eggs and supplied the wants of the nestlings; but at night if I looked at the nest by the aid of a lantern, the mother alone was sitting, and no peering or shaking of the branches revealed the perch of the father. This seemed a little unusual, as in the case of others of the same family, the wood thrush and the catbird, I had seen the male perch on the edge of the nest, on a twig near by, or huddling close to the female.

One bright moon-lit June night, chancing to go near the pines in the loneliest part of the garden, a hubbub arose as some night bird flapped in among the branches, and there sounded the rapid "quick! quick!" of alarm from a score or two of robins. But daylight did not reveal the trace of a nest in these pines, and after much watching and debating, I discovered that the birds which congregated there nightly were males, who gathered from sundown until an hour or so after, and roosted while their mates guarded the nests.

Bradford Torrey has noted this trait at length, with many interesting details, telling of roosts where the robins troop in nightly by hundreds, from a widely extended region; but this roost was in a garden where there were many passers, and seemed like a most exclusive coterie, or a very select bit of clubdom. They continued roosting in this way until early July, when, joined by their young, they disappeared for a time.

Have you ever noticed the oriole's fleetness of wing, foot, and eye? He is the fiery hang-bird who, wearing Lord Baltimore's colours, flits about among the sweeping elm branches in May, searching for a wand both strong and supple, where he may safely anchor his sky cradle. There is much thought required in the choosing of a location, with a dense leafy spray above it like an umbrella, and no twigs underneath to chafe when the wind rocks.

Near here is a garden, arched by elms and beeches, where all the season the most gorgeous flowers blaze upon the even turf, from the gold of the first crocus until the last chrysanthemum yields to the frost, and even then glass-shielded orchids and a mist of ferns and regal roses bridge the winter. The keeper of this garden lives with the flowers, watching the signs of sky and bird, and at night follows the moths with his net and lantern, and he told me this story of an oriole's power of thought.

Late in May, three pairs of orioles were locating their nests in the garden elms and there had been much skirmishing, fighting, and singing. Suddenly there arose a wonderful noise and commotion. Robins were giving the alarm to the bluebirds, thrushes, and sparrows, for high in the fork of a branch, a female oriole, who had slipped or was caught in flying, hung by the neck. Near by sat the three males, more quiet than agitated, while the other birds dashed about in the wildest excitement. The females cried, hovering about their unfortunate sister, pulling and jerking her tail, yet only succeeding in wedging her still more firmly. At last a gorgeous male darted up, and with wings spread dropped quickly on the forking prison, and with feet braced seized the choking bird by the neck with his beak, with one jerk releasing her, unhurt save for the loss of some feathers.

How the bird colours ebb and flow from spring until autumn! The grays of March and April are glinted by flying colour, though the earliest birds are more soberly clad than those that arrive when the leafage has grown. Wise Mother Nature, to drape your scouts in browns and russets with a dash of sky-blue or bark-green! How would the tanager, oriole, redstart, the chat and Maryland yellow-throat, or the bouquet of warblers escape the birds of prey, if when they came they found only bare branches? And the great, gold, swallow-tailed butterflies also, with the blue, the brick-red, and the variegated Apollo, reign in the torrid months, when their bird enemies have mostly gone northward, and they share the garden with the humming-bird.

The humming-bird hides his nest, or rather conceals it, by a trick of construction, which blends the nest with the branch, binding the soft bed of fern-wool and lichens to it so closely that the eye passes it over, and I seldom have found more than one nest in a season, though the flocks of parents and young gave indications of at least a dozen. In a nest that I saw this year, saddled aslant on a drooping beech bough, were two little hummers, a day or so from the egg, who bore hardly a bird-like feature, looking like tiny black beans pricked over with stiff dark bristles, but in two weeks they were wearing their iridescent coats of mail.

What becomes of the father birds, with their wonderful ruby gorgets, after the young are reared? All through July and August the birds have lived in the garden and swarmed in flocks about the sweet peas, carnations, and Japanese lilies, but I have never seen a ruby throat among them since the nesting time. In middle July, when I was training a vine to the arbour, a flock of humming-birds flew so close that I could have touched them with my hand. Contrary to their restless habits, they frequently perched on the trellis, and with a swift circular motion of the tongue licked the aphis from the curled edges of the leaves. They were newly fledged young wearing the female colours, as many birds do in their babyhood, but differing from their mothers in their lack of endurance, in a soft and infantile roundness, and in a total absence of fear. The old birds seldom alight, and I have seen one return from a dizzy flight and cover her nest without even grazing the margin. Sometimes the flock would number thirty or forty, and all the summer from dawn until sunset they fed in the garden, uttering harsh little cries, whirling and fighting, and only yielding their haunt to the hawk-moths at dusk. When there came with September some few days of dark, stormy weather, they circled high in excitement, and the next morning, as a flock, they had passed to the south, though a few stragglers remained all through October.

On the top of the trellis where the humming-birds and butterflies gathered, in a blaze of July sunshine, was a young cowbird. It did not perch, it sat, its only comprehension seeming to be the possession of a stomach, and the only sound it made was a sort of wheezing. At its side, a little beneath, was the nest of a chipping sparrow, the alien egg in its nest being one of the commonest tales of birdland sociology. The little sparrow, however, seemed proud of the rank, ungainly offspring, and lavished special care upon it, stretching on tiptoe to give the food that its size demanded, while her own nestlings, hungry and meagre, clamoured feebly. The cowbird typifies matter and craft, a dangerous conjunction, and the sparrow a case where scant sense is entirely subservient to the maternal instinct; tragedies that are not alone of the nest arise from such combinations.

The swallows distrusted the new barn; perhaps the paint startled them, or the slope of the eaves was inconvenient, and the glazed hay-loft window repelled them. In a few years the paint grew dim and weather-stained, crysalids hung in the groovings, and the glazed sash was left down to air the hay, so that its sweets, floating out, reassured them. In June a belated pair were looking for lodgings, and the outside not satisfying them, they ventured in at the window and busied themselves with a minute examination of every beam and rafter, prying here and there and peering about with the gait of woodpeckers. Then they attempted a nest, and all one day brought clay, with which, together with hay-straws, they moulded a bracket; but the second day it fell all in a lump, the smooth wood having in some way upset their plan of adhesion. They began another tour of inspection, and they found a support that was made of mellow old timber, sound and firm, but with a rough cuticle which absorbed more quickly and to which the clay stuck firmly. Here they again essayed, and in two days they had really completed their building.

The brood was ready to fly one warm day in the early part of August, or the parents at least thought so, but the nestlings were perfectly content where they were; the table was good and the view unexceptional. Coaxing did not avail, so next day the parents relentlessly pushed them out on the hay, and there they stayed for two days more. But they either could not or would not fly, and seemed to have cramps in their claws and weak ankles (tarsi is the more accurate term). The third day the parents refused to come further in than the window-sill, where they uttered a lisping chirp, fluttered their wings, and held out insects temptingly. In this way the young were lured up, and finally spent the night on the sill, cuddled together.

Next morning the wind blew sharply and the perch was disagreeable and draughty, so with encouraging cries the youngsters were coaxed to the limbs of a hemlock, the nearest tree to the window, but one which offered only a perilous footing. Two of the four found rest in the most steady branches, but two grasped bending twigs and swung over head downward, having no strength of grip with which to regain an upright position. Under one bird were tiers of soft green branches, under the other a stone wall, rough and jagged. The old birds gave a few sibilant twitters and darted invisibly high; in a minute or two the sky was alive with swallows, fluttering about the bird who was suspended over the wall; so many swallows had not been seen this season in all the village. To and fro they wheeled, keeping always above the little one, as if to attract its attention. The parents stayed nearer, and the mother held a moth in her beak and seemed to urge an effort to secure it. In a few minutes the bird who hung over the branches, relaxing his hold, turned, and spreading his wings slightly dropped to the branch beneath, where he settled himself comfortably.

Still above the wall the other hung motionless, except that its head was slowly drooping backward, and the circling birds grew more vociferous. Suddenly the parent who held the butterfly lit on the branch at the spot where the bird was clinging, and its mate darted swiftly close beneath.

Whether the darting bird really pushed the little one up, or only made the rush to startle it to sudden action, I could not discover, but in a flash the deed was accomplished and the bird righted and led into a bushy cover. The visiting swallows wheeled and lisped for a minute, and then were engulfed by the sky as mist in the air blends with the sunlight.

Tell me, positive science, were these manœuvres merely instinctive? Or, if you cannot, then confess bravely that there are things that you may not fathom.

Nature's Calm

The mountain brows, the rocks, the peaks are sleeping,
  Uplands and gorges hush!
The thousand moorland things are stillness keeping;
  The beasts under each bush
  Crouch, and the hivèd bees
  Rest in their honeyed ease;
In the purple sea fish lie as they were dead,
And each bird folds his wing over his head.

  —ALCMAN (Edwin Arnold's trans.)

The Great Oak

THE end of day. Sounds soften as the wind, their messenger, dies away; heat lessens as the sun gathers up his shafts before disappearing; dew glistens as the coolness holds down the moisture; then a twilight interlude of shadows. Shadows that roll groundward, cloud shadows drifting through the sun smoke, clasping the horizon with their clinging fingers; shadows of evening melody, shadows of pine fragrance, until all the shadows gather to line the sky arch and make it night.

The day is too short for the labours and pleasures crowding it, so that it would borrow time from the night; but night has need of its own hours, for sleeping Nature has its moods and attributes as well as Nature waking. When the warring day forces are at rest, and their star-angled differences converged, then in quiet may we look upon our mother earth, may hear her voices, and see in waking dreams the pictures that man can never chain to canvas as he does the things of day.

Day is relentless, boundless, pushing in its thoughts and suggestions; one road opens upon another and every path has its branches. Walk in the fields; at each step you meet a new circumstance and a different idea is forced upon you. In the woods you are led by a strange leaf, a new flower, a mossed stone,—in themselves trifles,—into infinite mental detail. The flight of a bird opens vista upon vista, until you cease to follow, cease even to absorb, but are both possessed and absorbed by the power of Nature. Beauty becomes almost an oppression, and the sun-fed colour blinding, the sense of personal littleness humbling. How can we realize it all, how can we arrange ourselves in relation to it and interpret it rightly? There is so much to see, so much to learn, and so little time between the first consciousness of the eye and its closing.

Night comes: a boundary is fixed above and around us; the horizon draws nearer; we are no longer at large, but surrounded, protected. It is a time of confidences; the migrating bird reveals to night the purpose of its silent journey, and the sleeping bird draws the darkness doubly close with his veiling wing. The flowers drowse in various attitudes, and man, in peace, may reconcile his tripartite nature, body, mind, and soul. Outside his door is the vast stage, well set with scenes for the revolving night-drama; the orchestra is ready; the Will-o'-the-wisp, the moon, the northern Aurora, and the piercing winter stars,—man only needs to send his fancy out to set all moving.

The first scene of the winter night-world is the sky above the window. When it is cloudless the constellations pace across it, but when clouded it is fathomless. Nowadays science teaches the places of the stars by lines and angles, but to those who when children studied the old black charts, with the strange figures of mythology enclosing their component stars outlined in white, the heavens are more vitally peopled. We cannot all be positive scientists, and heaven help the world if we could be! the spirit of things would be dried away by letter, and the affections ranged in systems about material suns.

From Indian summer until the vernal equinox is the time when vision most tends skyward. The Pleiad sisters lead the Milky Way in its scarf dance, and Taurus, with the star Aldebaran set in his forehead, follows Orion, the night-watchman, with his belt and club, who wears Betelgeuse for a shoulder knot. Below Orion, Canis Major trots backward, holding Sirius, for a lantern, in his jaws, and to the east Gemini, the smiling twins, walk in the Milky Way. In the northern sky the star-tailed Ursa Major points to Polaris, and southeastward Bootes leads his hounds, Asterion and Chara, as he drives the great star herds, almost touching with his spear Corona Borealis, the crown that Bacchus gave to Ariadne.

Under the stars the world seems closed, outline, not substance, and the clear, frosty sky a thing apart, of long ago, the region of gods and goddesses. When the earth, waking again, breathes gently, and the faint haze dims the electric winter clearness, Pan stirs in his sleep and raises to his lips his pipe, all choked with snow, and it gives forth a crackling purr, the first peep of the marsh hylode, and at this sound the sky draws again towards the earth and becomes a tributary.

Go out into the March night. The rough wind rattles against the blinds; there are snow patches in the garden and snow banks under the north fences. The leaves still rustling on the honeysuckle are answered by those that the winter's hail has failed to beat from the oaks and beeches; but when the tender buds come, they will do what force could not do, and the withered leaves will fall away, as Death's fetters drop before the touch of immortality.

You hear the same sounds as of the past months: the creakings of tree trunks and of boughs, the sparrows fidgeting in their perch under the piazza eaves, and perhaps an owl quavering in the old chestnut. Yet there is a sense of change, a different quality to the air, and more, for two new sounds separate themselves from all the others. The river, freed from ice, is rushing over the milldam, and the hylodes are peeping faintly.

Daylight did not show even an early bee, though for a week wood has been sawed in a sunny spot and the sweet dust lies scattered on the ground; but through the night, from the warm southeast, where the sun first touches the fields that run to the marshes, where there are old matted reeds, comes the welcome "peep! peep! peep!" As the days lengthen, from afternoon till dawn you hear the marsh frogs' chorus; it is not musical and would be little prized at any other season. Surely the hylodes, more than the larger frogs, inspired Aristophanes by their ceaselessness:—

> In their yearly revelry,
> Brékeke—késh, ko-ásh, ko-ásh!

But this croaking makes the blood flow quicker; it is the vocal spring sign of animal nature, even though the fox and owl may breed in February, and it is the prophet of the coming bird music even as the skunk-cabbage is the forerunner of the violet. The late March moon has a more human face, though it still casts bare shadows, and as it pales at morning the song-sparrows huddled in the bushes sing half to the night and half to the day.

The typical spring night is only quiet in comparison to dawn and twilight. Even-song lasts an hour after sundown and matins begin as long before sunrise. Even in the midnight hours, the forces of Nature are too potent to rest wholly; in this lies the principal difference between the nights of spring and those of early autumn. The temperature of the two seasons is much alike, and the shadows also, but the spring nights overflow with little murmurings. Birds stir and change their perching, and with drowsy bustle flutter from branch to branch; the whip-poor-will awakes the wood echoes, and his cry never grows too familiar to lend a touch of mystery to common things. A veery, suddenly awakened, thinks the moon the sun and sings a few dreamy notes, and a startled robin calls "quick! quick!" in alarm. The great green pond frogs call out unblushingly, "d-r-r-r-unk! d-r-r-r-unk!" and the swifts, rising from their chimney nests with whirling wings, make mimic thunder. The brooks and the river run at freshet speed, and the sound coming unmuffled by walls of leaves seems at the door; the tide measures its height upon the beach with ringing strokes.

As darkness limits the range of the eye, the senses of ear and nose grow keener, and the denser night air intensifies both sound and perfume. If you should start in quest of the little screech-owl, that seems to call from the cedars near by, you will need magic boots to take you across the wet meadows before you will find him; and the cloying fragrance that envelops the porch in reality comes from the beds of hyacinths down in the garden.

The autumn night has few voices, and fewer perfumes. There are no pond frogs, and the hylode's peep is exchanged for the dryer chirp of crickets. The whip-poor-will is gone and the night-hawk also; the owl remains persistently and mingles his infrequent hooting with the cries of wild ducks and geese signalling the way to salt water; while the essence of decaying vegetation is the only perfume.

What wonderful pictures the moon sketches in black and white! she is the universal artist. In winter she etches on a plate of snow, biting deeply the branch shadows, retouching with twig dry-point all the bones of things, Nature's anatomy. In spring, she broadens her work to a soft mezzotint, and then on to india-ink washes and sepia groundings. First, the outlined catkin, then leaf forms; next, simply draped branches, and then to complete, though rapid, compositions. The May-fly then hums every night among the wood-fragrant flowers of the lindens, the grass has grown high, the wind-flower hangs its closed petals, and the scouring-rush, strung with dewdrops, equals the diamond aigrette of an empress. The moon-pictures deepen and expand as the shadows grow more dense, until they become intelligible, impressionistic, and truth-telling.

The drama of the summer night follows, with times of Egyptian darkness, when the woods are thick with a blackness that overpowers reason itself. The air is heavy with sleeplessness; the earth teems with form, life, and colour. The sky is subservient to this beauty; the moon is a lamp to reveal it, and shares its domain with the lightning; for now we do not look so much at the moon as at what the moon shows us.

The full-leaved trees make cavernous shadows, and the meadows, silvered with dew, seem like enchanted lakes. Every strip of woods becomes a Black Forest, the tall grass and brakes are jungles, the cat crouching through them a tiger, and the bats soaring witches. The lane seems endless, the trimmed hemlocks solidify into a fortress, the pool where the birds bathe looks bottomless. The leaves of the water-lily lie heavily; the iris blades, steeled with dew, rise like the spears of engulfed knights. The frogs keep up a fitful groaning; the sharp-slanting moon-streaks shoot across the dell like search-lights, unravelling a mystery. Moisture drips from the fern fronds, and where old tree stumps have lain a long time on the ground, a night village has sprung up. The gypsy race of plant-land has reared its fungus encampment, with wide white tents and peaked brown pagodas, where the flat glow-worm is the general manager. Motes and great moths float on the path made by the moon's rays,—

> Or, weird and wee, sits Puck himself,
> With legs akimbo, on a fern?

Have you ever watched the flower world asleep? In the fields the clover clasps its leaves like clenched fists; the wayside partridge-pea shuts its leaflets into a clasp-knife, resembling its seed-pod. The ox-eye daisy droops its head and faces the sunset, but turns until it again faces the sun at dawn. The wild aster tribe curl their ray flowers into little bundles, and the blue gentian closes its fringed eyelids.

In the garden some sleep and some are awake. The poppy closes to a pilgrim's cockle-shell, just as the evening primrose spreads its green-gold salvers; the eglantine simply curls in its petals, as do also the single rose and the blackberry. The calendulas draw their rays into a stack, and the sturdy lupins drop their leaflets or sometimes shoot them up like reversed umbrellas. The moon-flower, the white ipomea, opens in rivalry a planetary system of its own with the green trellis for an orbit.

The sweet peas contract rather than close; the single Dahlias lose their rigidity, and almost all single flowers, missing the sun's stimulus, twist or droop. Even the vagrant pusley, with palm pressed to palm, prays the night wind for pity on its despised estate. The morning-glories hold to dawn their wine cups, drinking night out and crying wassail to morning. In what factory of crystal was their translucence fashioned? Were they concealed in some treasure-laden tomb of Nineveh? Did Venice foster them, or is their beauty wholly Bohemian? Who dreamed their shaping, melting wide rainbows for their colouring? Who poised them on their standards? Was it Palissy? No! simply Nature, whose workshop sends out all incomparable things, fashioned them to meet Aurora's pledging lips.

The fragrance of the Virgin's lilies pierces you through and through; the honeysuckle odour clings and overwhelms the heliotrope until the mignonette seems almost a stimulant by contrast. The rose-bed scatters scented petals, and the buds of yesterday relax the grip of the green calyx, only waiting for the sun's expanding touch.

Beyond the marshes the sea-sands do not blind the eyes as in the daytime, but cool, gray, and sparkling with mica, they blend with the sky and water, while the lighthouse eyes wink wisely. Across the sky and the water down to your feet stretches the path of the moon, scintillating and drawing you to it, obliterating everything else and bridging space by its magnetism. Step in the current; the black tide looks solid; you marvel the feet can move through it. Wade further in; up the water creeps as you advance. Swim! the cold and resistance seem to lessen as you cleave the liquid moonlight. It is a different world, yourself and Nature, yourself and space, with self a pigmy in it. A white-sailed boat dives through the silver and breaks the enchantment; how cold the water grows again in spite of the languor of the summer night!

The sea-breeze rolls the mist over the meadows, until it envelops both plain and village in soft folds of tulle; the church steeple emerges above it, and the distant hills are islands, with strange cloud-shapes hanging above them. What flocks and herds graze in the pastures of the sky, now following the moon and then flying from it! The black-edged wind-clouds are Southdown sheep disturbed by a shadow, and then a herd of brown buffaloes gallop across, a trail of mist dust following. A desert caravan crawls close to the horizon, and on the earth the shadows sharpen and the pointed cedars take weird shapes like those which Doré portrayed haunting the Wandering Jew.

All these things of the night pass in a little space, and man may gather and arrange them to suit his needs; for the body, sleep; for the mind, peace; for the soul, a clearer vision. It was night that brought to the hillside shepherds the vision of the Bethlehem Star.

The Story
of a Garden

Nature, as far as in her lies,
Imitates God, ...

—TENNYSON, "On a Mourner"

The Flower Corner

There is a garden that is not like the other gardens round about. In many of these gardens the flowers are only prisoners, forced to weave carpets on the changeless turf, and when the eye is sated and the impression palls, they become to their owners, who have no part in them, merely purchased episodes.

This garden that I know has a bit of green, a space of flowers, and a stretch of wildness, as Bacon says a garden should always have. At its birth the twelve months each gave to it a gift, that it might always yield an offering to the year, and presently it grew so lovable that there came to it a soul.

The song-sparrow knows that this is so; the mottled owl that lives in the hollow sassafras has told it to the night-hawk. Catbirds and robins, routed from other gardens by fusillades, still their quick-throbbing hearts, feeling its protection. The coward crow alone knows its exclusion, for he was unhoused from the tall pines and banished for fratricide. The purling bluebird, claiming the pole-top house as an ancestral bequest, repeats the story every springtime. The oriole and swallow whisper of it in their southward course, and, returning, bring with them willing colonists.

The rock polypody creeps along in confidence, with no ruthless hand to strip it off, and the first hepatica opens its eyes in safety, for tongues of flame or the grub-axe have not crippled it during the winter. Once the petted garden beauties looked askance, from their smooth beds in the tilled corner, and drew their skirts away from the wildwood company, but now, each receiving according to its need, they live in perfect concord.

The wild rose in the chinky wall peeps shyly at her glowing sisters, and the goldenrod bows over it to gossip with the pentstemon. And this is how it came to be, for the garden was no haphazard accident. Nature began it, and, following her master-touch, the hand and brain of a man, impelled by a reverent purpose, evolved its shaping.

This man, even when a little boy, had felt the potency of Nature's touch to soothe the heartache. One day, led by an older mate, he trudged a weary way to see a robber hanged. The child, not realizing the scene he was to witness, was shocked to nervous frenzy, and a pitying bystander, thinking to divert his mind, gave him a shilling. Spying a bird pedlar in the crowd, he bought a goldfinch and a pint of seeds, and the horror of the hanging was quite forgotten and effaced by the little bird, his first possession. To it he gave his confidence and told all his small griefs and joys, and through the bird Nature laid her warm hand on his heart and gently drew it toward their mutual Master, and never after did he forget her consolation.

All this was more than seventy years ago. When the boy grew to manhood, following the student life, the spirit of the bird that had blotted out the scene of civil murder was still with him. Its song kept his thoughts single and led him toward green fields, that their breath might leaven lifeless things, strengthening the heart that felt a world-weariness, as all must feel at times when facing human limitations.

Love came, and home; then, following hand in hand, honour and disappointment; and again, with double purpose, he turned Nature-ward. Not to the goatish Pan, but to Nature's motherhood, to find a shrine upon her breast where he might keep his holiest thoughts, and watch them grow. A place apart, where the complete man might be at rest, and walking in the cool of day feel the peace of God.

At first the garden was a formless bit of waste, but Nature tangles things with a motive, and it was in the making that it came to win a soul, for the man's spirit grew so calm and strong that it gave its overplus to what it wrought.

The garden's growth was nowhere warped or stunted by tradition; there was no touch of custom's bondage to urge this or that. No rudeness had despoiled its primal wildness, and lovers, who had trodden paths under the trees, were its sole discoverers. It was rock-fenced and briar-guarded; the sharp shadows of the cedars dialed the hours, and the ground-pine felt its darkened way beneath them with groping fingers.

This happened before I was, but hearing of it often, sound has imparted its sense to sight, and it all seems visual. With my first consciousness, the days were filled with planting and with growth; the pines already hid the walls, and cattle tracks were widened into paths and wound among young maples, elms, and beeches. Then there grew in me a love that made the four garden walls seem like the boundaries of the world.

Nothing was troubled but to free it from the oppression of some other thing. The sparrow kept his bush, and between him and the hawkheadsman a hand was raised. The wood thrush, finding his haunts untouched, but that his enemies, the black snakes, might no longer boldly engulf his nestlings, raised his clear voice and sang "O Jubilate Deo!" The gardener who planted no longer watches the bird's flight, but the garden still tells its story. Will you come in? The gate is never closed except to violence.

Eight acres of rolling ground, and in the centre a plainly cheerful house decides the point of view. The location of a house much affects the inmates; here sunshine penetrates every room and a free current of air sweeps all about, and there is a well of sparkling water close at hand. This well is rock-drilled, deep and cold, and the patron divinity of all good wells, the north star, watches over it, and nightly Ursa Major's dipper circles above, as if offering a cooling draught to all the constellations.

For a space about the house the grass is cropped, and some plump beds of geraniums, Fuchsias, heliotropes, serve to grade the eye from indoor precision, to rest the vision before the trees and moving birds compel it to investigation. However much natural wildness may soothe and satisfy, the home is wholly a thing of man's making, and he may gather about it the growing things that need his constant ministry. The sight of such an open space gives the birds more confidence, and the worm enemies that always follow cultivation offer them a change of food.

The old queen-apple tree that casts its petals every May against the window-panes, like snow blushing at its own boldness, held many nests last spring. A bluebird spied a knot-hole where decay had left him an easy task; a pair of yellow warblers, with cinnamon-streaked breasts, fastened their tiny cup between a forked branch above the range of sight. For several days I watched these birds, fluttering about the window corners where cobwebs cling and spiders weave, and thought they searched for food, until, following the yellow flash they made among the leaves, I saw that they were building; and when I secured the empty nest in August, it proved to be a dainty thing woven of dry grass, the down of dandelions, cocoons, and cobwebs.

A robin raised two broods, building a new nest for the second, as the first one was too near the path to suit his partner's nerves. He spent his days in prying earth-worms from the lawn, singing at dawn and twilight so deliciously that he furnished one more proof that bird voices, even of the same species, have individual powers of expression, like those of men.

The fourth bird to build, a red-eyed vireo, was quite shy at first, yet hung the nest over the path, so that when I passed to and fro her ruby eyes were on a level with me. After the eggs were laid, she allowed me to bend down the branch, and a few days later, to smooth her head gently with my finger. A chipping sparrow added his wee nest to the collection, watching the horses as they passed, timidly craving a hair from each, and finally securing a tuft from an old mattress, with which he lined his home to his complete content.

If you would keep the wild birds in your garden, you must exclude from it four things: English sparrows, the usual gardeners, cats, and firearms. These sparrows, even if not belligerent, are antagonistic to song birds, and brawl too much; a cat of course, being a cat, carries its own condemnation; a gun aimed even at a target brings terror into bird-land; and a gardener, of the type that mostly bear the name, is a sort of bogyman, as much to Nature lovers as to the birds. The gardener wishes this, orders that, is rigid in point of rights and etiquette, and looks with scarcely veiled contempt at all wild things, flowers, birds, trees; would scrape away the soft pine needles from the footpaths and scatter stone dust in their place, or else rough, glaring pebbles. He would drive away the songsters with small shot, his one idea of a proper garden bird being a china peacock.

It is, of course, sadly true, that cherries, strawberries, grapes, and hungry birds cannot meet with safety to the fruit, but we should not therefore emulate the men of Killingworth. We may buy from a neighbouring farmer, for a little money, all the fruit we lack, but who for untold gold can fill the hedge with friendly birds, if once we grieve or frighten them away?

You may grow, however, tender peas in plenty, and all the vegetables that must go direct from earth to table to preserve their flavour; only remember when you plant the lettuce out, to dedicate every fourth head to the wild rabbits, who, even while you plant, are twitching their tawny ears under the bushes, and then you will suffer no disappointment. Once in a time a gardener-naturalist may drift to you, and your garden will then entertain a kindred spirit. Such a man came to this garden, a young Dane, full of northern legend and sentiment, recognizing through rough and varied work the motive of the place,—like drawing like; and with him, a blonde-haired, laughing wife, and a wee daughter called Zinnia, for the gay flowers, and he found time to steal among the trees in the June dawns to share in the bird's raptures, making his life in living.

It is a drowsy August afternoon; the birds are quiet, and the locusts express the heat by their intonation. The Japan lilies, in the border back of the house, are densely sweet, the geraniums mockingly red, and the lemon-verbena bushes are drooping. The smooth grass and trim edges stop before an arch that spans the path, and about it shrubs straggle, grouping around a tall ash. This ash, a veritable lodestone to the birds, is on the borderland of the wild and cultivated, and they regard it as the Mussulman does his minaret, repairing there to do homage. Before the leaves appear the wood thrush takes the topmost branch to sing his matins, as if, by doing so, he might, before his neighbours, give the sun greeting.

The robins light on it, *en route*, when they fear that their thefts in other gardens will find them out, and the polite cedar-birds, smoothing each other's feathers, sun themselves in it daily before the flocks break into pairs. Upon the other side, a hospitable dogwood spreads itself, a goodly thing from spring till frost, and from it spireas, Deutzias, weigelas, lilacs, the flowering quince, and strawberry shrub, follow the path that winds under the arch, past mats of ferns and laurel, to a tilled corner, a little inner garden, where plants are nursed and petted, and no shading tree or greedy root robs them of sun or nourishment.

Along the path between the pines, the black leaf mould of the woods has been strewn freely. The fern tribe is prolific in this neighbourhood, and a five-mile circuit encloses some twenty species, most of which may be transplanted, if you keep in mind their special needs. This spot is cool and shady, but the soil is dry from careful drainage. The aspidiums flourish well; *A. acrostichoides*, of two varieties, better known as the Christmas fern, with heavy varnished fronds, *A. marginale*, with pinnate, dull-green fronds, *A. cristatum*, almost doubly pinnate and with them the fragrant *Dicksonia punctilobula*, whose straw-coloured lace carpets the autumn woods with sunlight, and the black-stemmed maidenhair grows larger every year, rearing its curving fronds two feet or more.

What endless possibilities creep into the garden with every barrow of wood earth! How many surprises cling about the roots of the plant you hope to transfer uninjured from its home! Bring a tuft of ferns, lo! there springs up a dozen unseen things—a pad of partridge vine, an umber of ginseng, a wind flower; in another year the round leaves of the pyrola may appear and promenade in pairs and trios quite at their ease, until the fern bed becomes a constant mystery. For many years some slow awaking seeds will germinate, the rarer violets, perhaps an orchis.

I brought a mat of club moss, with a good lump of earth, as was my habit, from the distant woods. Several years after, happening to stop to clear away some dead branches, I started in surprise, for enthroned in the centre of the moss, a very queen, was a dark pink cypripedium, the Indian moccasin. It is an orchid very shy of transposition, seldom living over the second season after its removal, seeming to grieve for its native home with the fatal Heimweh, so that the seed must have come with the moss and done its growing in the fern nook.

Do you hear that hoarse call—kuk-kuk-kuk? Above are a pair of yellow-billed cuckoos, with ashy breasts, brown backs warming in colour toward the tail and on the wings, and with powerful beaks. They have little in common with the European cuckoo, being, though less beautiful, superior in morality, and our greatest protector against the tent-worm. They promised last May, in return for shelter, to clear the orchard of this pest, and they kept faith. Day after day they worked, tearing the wormy films apart in very wantonness and not for food, though before the caterpillars came the cuckoo was almost a stranger.

Come into the rustic shelter that overlooks the flower corner. The cedars that make it were born upon the soil, and the bitter-sweet vine around the entrance is their old acquaintance. On the right is the sparrows' hedge, dense, and full eight feet wide, and the sparrows claim it from attic to cellar and grow quite pert in their security. The flower corner faces west and south; a few hours later you may see the sun go down behind the hills, and the bright colours of the flowers focus the eye for sunset glories. This shelter is a place for twilight hours. The vesper-sparrow comes here, and the veery haunts the trees that follow a watercourse down in the meadow; and together they perform a duet—flute and flageolet—while the spiders, crawling out as the darkness deepens, trace their webs to and fro, to and fro, drop a stitch, pick up a stitch—crafty knitters!

This flower corner hears the call of spring before its messenger has penetrated the woodlands. *Daphne mezereum*, touched by early sunbeams, shows its pink clusters in March, and starts the glad procession before even the hepatica has stirred, and the sweet white violets often open where the sun has made dimples in the snow. This little close yields a posy every day, from March until in late November it offers the last pansy as a thought of all the season's beauty, and even in snow and ice a few sashed frames hold a store of blooming violets, to keep spring in the heart.

You saw the garden when on May-day, bleak and chilly, the bulb-growths wrapped it in colour; then when the quaint border beauties followed, and when the roses rioted, and after their brief festival left the earth strewn with the perfumed tatters of their leaves. Now those rose trees yield a pleasant aftermath to mingle with the scentless autumn flowers.

The asters of all hues and forms make solid banks of colour; the tall Dahlias, precise and quilled, carry out the scheme, going into lighter fancies with the more graceful single blooms. There is a ponderous majesty in these precursors of the chrysanthemum, a weight of velvets following the laces and silks of the earlier season.

The latest garden gift, the Margaret carnation, brings with it every shade and tint, giving a refreshing spiciness to the bouquet, and mignonette always lives out its name. The simple borders are so fashioned that they have their seasons like wild Nature,—spring, summer, autumn, and even in winter they wear a quilt of leaves and cheerful cedar boughs.

Walk down with me to the seat beside the honeysuckle trellis. On the right is a wall of green, and under the arched spruces goes the lane walk. The lane is shady with a wood dimness, and from it stray dogwood, red-berried elder, white thorn, birch, clethra, sumach, oak, and sassafras. This is Thrush Lane; here the hermit thrush comes in May, and in October returns to feed on the wedge-shaped magnolia berries. Here the brown thrasher scratches and rustles daily and the wood thrush stays to nest, while the olive-backed and gray-cheeked thrushes make semi-annual visits. The catbird and the sociable robin find the lane too dull except for noon siestas, but the warblers love it for the shelter and the food it yields them.

Between the bushes, in little gaps, the elm-leaved goldenrod, the silver rod, wild sunflowers, and asters are now opening. Where the sun breaks through, before the turn, you see the path line is carried out with shrubs, snowballs, bush-honeysuckle, tamarix, cotoneaster, barberry, and many others. In a clearing, where the ground rolls to some apple trees, the mulberry, mountain ash, and a choke-cherry tree were planted especially for the benefit of the birds, and the rough old willow, too, is surrounded by young hawthorns, where the hair-bird likes to build. See! all through the stubbly orchard grass run pale green ribbons of the sensitive fern, and in another month the bronze-fronded moonwort will follow them.

Up hill a bit, the pines and spruces meet you, the rocks break through the scanty soil; in fact, the garden, like some hillside vineyards, is founded on a rock, the soil being deep only in pockets. This is all the better for wood things that love chinks and crannies; and the evergreens flourish, having the knack of running out their roots like anchors.

How much we owe to these same evergreens, beautiful and protective at all times, in all seasons! Snow-feathered they give a Christmas gladness to the landscape, then pink-tipped in their blooming time before putting on their fresh green summer plumes; in autumn filling the sudden emptiness, waving warning arms to drive the cold from all the tender things that creep or fly into their shelter. The hemlock, ever faithful, breaks the fury of the north wind; the Scotch pine sends out warmth from its ruddy bark; the white pine emerges from the morning mist, shaking diamonds from its drenched locks, and in autumn drops them like elfin straws to make a winter thatch for all the little colonies in the earth. The pines are cheerful and strong, even from the tiny seedling piercing the moss:—

> First a little slender line,
> Like a mermaid's green eyelash, and then anon
> A stem a tower might rest upon,
> Standing spear-straight in the waist-deep moss,
> Its bony roots clutching around and across,
> As if they would tear up earth's heart in their grasp
> Ere the storm should uproot them or make them unclasp:
> Its cloudy boughs singing as suiteth the pine.

Even the juniper that spreads itself in the pasture gives the same pledge to the fields that the witch-hazel gives to the woods. Under the trees on each side of the path the pipsissewa raises its rigid leaves, and the fruit even now is reddening on the partridge vine. Go up the three stone steps to the resting-place between the shaggy hickories. It is so high that the outlook is through the branches. It is a perch where the birds are neighbours, and the red squirrels leap from branch to roof, forward and back, and the chipmunk crawls through a knot-hole in the floor to quizz you, and then pours out a wrathful volley at your intrusion.

In October it is good to sit up here as the leaves fall with a soft monotony, such as water-ripples make, and closing the eyes one can hear the drift of the leafy tide, breaking in unhurried waves. In spring the rocks are red with columbines and the black birch gilds them with its pollen.

Look below! there lies the garden's eye, its heart of hearts, the pool, fed by a ceaseless spring and tingeing the ground about with emerald. What bird is there that does not claim it for his summer watering-place? When every other pond and many brooks are dry in this arid month of August, the pool remains, only shrinking a little at the margin, showing the stems of pickerel-weed and sagittaria. White water-lilies sway upon its surface; some are shut and others, in the last day of their flowerhood, are still open, as if reluctant to close their eyes on so much beauty. Sharp flag leaves break the edge, and tall Osmundas look over them to see their own reflections; *O. regalis*, the queen, who often wears in her pinnate fronds the mystic number thirteen; *O. cinnamomea*, whose leaves, wool-wrapped in youth, yield their fleece to line the nests of humming-birds and warblers; and straggling away from them is the common brake, alike of roadside, marsh, or clearing.

Beyond in the moist dell, where a hundred or two red-gold flower spikes glow, is a transplanted stranger, the barbaric yellow-fringed orchid of the sea-gardens, now quite at home, and its insect friends have found it, so that it seeds as freely as in its native marsh.

Another of the orchid tribe flourishes under the maples, the large yellow cypripedium, called in France, *le soulier de Notre Dame*; and in a dozen places, the little tway-blade, in June, throws up its purple-green flowers.

Watch the birds flutter and bathe on the flat shelving stones! Some evidently take a dozen baths a day. The great iridescent frogs swim lazily and the dragon-flies dart and flash; a tired dog, following a wagon on the highway, comes to the pool quite fearlessly and drinks with long laps of satisfaction.

Oaks, maples, chestnuts, shade a tranquil vista, lovely now, but fairer still in June, when the ox-eye daisies swept the shadowy dell with their sundance and the iris stepped a minuet between tall grasses.

In yonder arch of spruces, Dante stands carved in stone. The tempering mould and moss relax his stern features, set with the vision of human destiny. A glint of sunshine, passing across his face like a thought of Beatrice, illuminates it, and warms the lips to seeming speech:—

All *hate* abandon ye who enter here!

In truth this one small word is all the span between heaven and hell.

Rustling Wings

All the feathered airy nation,
   Birds of every size and station,
      Are convened in convocation.
   *   *   *   *   *   *   *   *   *

How they thicken, how they muster,
How they clutter, how they cluster!
Now they ramble here and thither,
Now they scramble all together.

—ARISTOPHANES, *The Birds* (Frere's trans.)

Maidenhair Fern

THE wood swallows began it and signalled the grackles, or perhaps the grackles, chattering in the trees, so jarred upon the nerves of the swallows that they fled to the dunes, where there are no echoes.

It was the first of September, and I was gathering sea-lavender on the borders of the marsh, where it had escaped the mowers. There was a great fluttering in the bayberries and sand-plum bushes; they bent and swayed, and the heavy-topped goldenrod quivered unreasonably. Becoming curious, I crept behind a trail of old rail fences toward the place, briers holding me back and all the weeds clutching at me with their desperate little seed claws. From the bushes the swallows darted, percussive, bolt-like, then spreading widely, flying by tens and hundreds, cutting the air with the scattering swiz-z-z of shot, followed by the smoke of intense vibration, until they seemed only a point in the distance, yet a punctuation point in the unbroken phrase of summer.

We are never ready for autumn, when the almanac doles out September. Mind and body are relaxed and expanded by the liberal juices of summer, the air above is still soft, the grass richly green, the eye filled with colour and focused for sunlight, the skin pores moist, respirative, and the house of the body unguarded. So Nature, never abrupt, sends a bird message—a gentle, unjarring reminder—to prepare the way, before a single tree shows the red flag of warning or a chilly breath contracts the muscles.

In this interval, when the commencement of the season's ebb-tide is scarcely perceptible, it is a sort of high noon. In the spring the eye went from the leafless trees to the birds, and then back to the trees, as the birds became hidden by their leafage. In this, the earth's middle season, as the great sap-ebbing begins, Nature draws the eye again to the birds, and these wandering minstrels play a comedy for those who will look at them, a sociological drama—name it, The Ideal Republic of Birdland.

As the birds change their plumage and drift, their companions, the leaves, soon follow, knowing that their protection is no longer needed.

Down on the dunes, the summer-bright first of September the wood swallows came, and we watch and wait and thrill as one by one the birds of spring return and in a motley dress flutter about us. Some come on night wings, others stop to rest at twilight, in flocks of a kind, by twos and threes, or in a straggling army together, all tribe barriers dropped, all social etiquette banished.

The blue sky and gold sun, filtered together, shoot green glints on the dunes, on the water, on the spume-edged tide pools, where the sandpipers patter and leave their sharp footprints; and there the wood swallows began the play, the waves lapping the overture. Hidden in the cover of sand plums, I waited to see what would happen. The volley that had flown over my head shifted, neared twice, then parted, and finally settled all around, with the sound that only wings or winds make, yes, even on the bunch of sea-lavender that I was holding.

The most startling thing was the flock impulse binding them together. In the spring an individual bird sings an individual song, and if you have keen ears you may detect that no two birds of a species have precisely the same intonation, and some birds, as the song-sparrow for instance, vary their theme until even their identity is puzzling. Each woos for himself an individual mate, with the exception of one or two vagabonds, and builds a particular nest, and wears a coat which marks both his sex and tribe. In autumn, the vital need of these things having passed, the characteristics in themselves are in a measure merged, and in the search for shelter and food the collective instinct holds sway.

These swallows did not feed, but merely twittered, and clung to small twigs, keeping their wings and tails in motion, as soldiers keep step when halting. For three or four minutes they rested, and then came another ascension, and as they flew over, their wing-beats gave me the same sensation as a pelting of small pebbles.

For three days I went to watch them, and finally decided that all the seemingly useless effort of flying and counterflying was, in fact, an initiation for the young in the fatigues and manœuvres of travel, a sort of awkward squad drill. On the first day some stragglers dropped from the column, some clung to the bushes and chirped in irresolution, but on the third day they flew as one swallow.

After this, an easterly storm prevailed and the marshes were flooded. Upon the seventh of September I went again to the beach, and was watching a fishhawk, who had twice lost his prey in mid-air, when a heap of metallic seaweed beyond me seemed to move, and, startled, I saw the swallows rise in a straight line, then angle and sweep over the Sound at a point west of south, and that was their last rehearsal.

I should like to know if they lingered on Long Island; for if they began their long southward journey, they travel by day, as their start was at ten o'clock in the morning.

Meanwhile the purple grackles, which reappeared the same day as the swallows, continued to forage in the pastures, and daily augmented their hosts. After the silence of late August, even their harsh cry is not disagreeable, but rather suggests that Nature's doors, so long open to sunshine and summer, though reluctant to close, are trying their rusty hinges. There is something quite exciting as, after much fussing and shifting, a flock of grackles settle down on the maples, and thence to the ground. These birds are extremely wary of alighting on any species of evergreen, and in this are a rare exception. I have watched them year after year, and though the place is surrounded by pines, spruces, and cedars, the birds seldom more than brush them in passing. The sun develops a wonderful iridescence in their sombre coats. They appear coal-black from beneath, but as they walk on the ground and the light strikes on their backs, purples, blues, and greens develop, coming to a focus in the yellow circle of the iris. Even in autumn, they are not always the ravenous corn-destroyers that they are reputed. I watched a flock in a newly ploughed field, where the ground was heavy and sour, full of grubs and evil larvæ, and the grackles went to work and for a week poked and gobbled, doing away with quantities of injurious insects.

The migratory range of birds appears to be a largely unsettled question. Do they go further north after nesting and return for a time in the autumn, or do the local birds merely retreat to the deep woods and then reappear? For myself, I think that here in southeastern Connecticut, many birds go further north and east in August, returning to their haunts in advance of the general migration.

It may be fancy perhaps, but I believe that I can distinguish the birds that have nested and brought out their young in the garden, from the strangers; there is something more friendly in those that have let me watch them, that have perched on my favourite arbour—surely they ought to be more confiding than the mere transients of passage. There are many birds that we never see here except during their migrations; an innumerable list, topped by the great fox-sparrow and dwindling to the ruby-crowned kinglet.

Two birds especially have lent me a key to the situation: a male robin with strange white markings on the back, as if hoar frost had clung to his feathers, and a catbird with a claw so crumpled that he hopped on the ankle.

These birds were quite tame and had nested close to the foot-path, so that I really had an intimate friendship with them. In early August I missed them, but when, during the second week of September, after some very rough weather, I was looking out early one morning at a small flock of robins, I saw my albino among them. In an hour or so, he was prying about in his garden haunts, with an inquiring air, to see what changes had occurred in his absence.

Another day we hung some bunches of half-ripe grapes on the boughs of a pear tree, and watched to see what birds would come to take them. Many catbirds had returned, pert as ever, but they had forgotten their songs, and the cool nights had stiffened their throats into mewing. These catbirds spied the grapes first, and the robins followed, taking the clusters away to eat at their leisure, and on the roof of the porch I distinguished my old friend with the crumpled claw.

Autumn's sky colours are very illusive; the smoky brown mist rising from the ground veils the most exquisite combinations. The songs of the adult birds, if the few disconnected notes may be called songs, touch chords wholly of reminiscence. I heard a fluty whistle coming from a tangle—instantly my thoughts receded. "If it was June," I said, "I should know that a chat was hiding there." All the while, this olive and gold recluse was perching close at hand, giving his call at intervals so softly, as if even to himself it was but the whisper of memory. The young birds, however, furnish by their little warblings one of the enchantments of autumn that is a forecast of spring rapture.

Go to some hollow or bushy nook not far remote from houses,—a garden seat in an arbour, or a stone by the spring, are perhaps the best places,—and when the surroundings have accustomed themselves to you, have accepted the honesty of your intentions so that you may move your head without causing any alarm, then you may listen to the babbling of the young birds of the season, the first sounds from the newly developed throats. These notes are so fresh and young, so sweet and guileless, wholly without emotion, like childish prattle, and in keeping with the birds' hybrid feathers. It is easy to tell the young from their experienced parents, even when there is nothing decisive in their plumage: they are less timid and gaze about in an unconcerned way, and their proportions have a callow roundness.

The old wrens now are silent, and seem transformed from the cheerful, fussy companions of June days, to sulky misanthropes. Listen to that roulade! low and uncertain, but one of the young is telling you how he will sing next May. After a few days spent with the autumnal bird flocks, you will decide that the call notes come from the old, but the scraps of song mostly from the young birds, and that such music as autumn yields is not so much a farewell as a prelude.

On the tenth of September the golden orioles came and swung in a trumpet vine, and a half dozen young ones dashed about in a fly-catcher way, lisping a little. The same day, the white-breasted nuthatch was climbing in the great white oak by the spring, performing numerous acrobatic feats, head downward, and announcing himself by his grating call. His note, a mere scrap of the jay's scream, associates him with those smartly dressed thieves, as their seasons of return are alike.

Now the birds come drifting steadily along; one morning will bring a flock of chestnut-crowned sparrows, and the next some brown thrashers, while a little later the towhee will be seen, hopping with nice precision. Is there any other bird to whom the word neat applies more truly than to this ground-robin, as we locally call him, with his trig build, his precise plumage and markings, and his thrifty, satisfied note?

The middle of the month, the flycatchers held a great rally in the top of a dead elm: the king-bird, though fearless, keeping the furthest aloof; the phœbes, the only ones of the tribe who carry a note of music, coming down to a pear tree where insects hover over the fallen fruit. The great crested flycatcher, with a nonchalant air of defiance, followed very cautiously the flight of the king-bird. The least flycatcher, with white eye-ring, gray-green back, and "chebec call" was the most sociable, and peered about the apple trees; his yellow-bellied cousin chose the trumpet vine for a point of vantage, and muttered its slow call in imitation of the wood-pewee. For many days these birds drew all attention to themselves by their eccentric ways, each choosing a separate foraging spot, but when disturbed, returning to the elm. They held the air in such absolute mastery that it seemed to represent both earth and water. They flew through it, next seemed to swim, then twisted and moved by jerks as if running on the ground. By the twenty-fifth of the month they had all disappeared, except the phœbes and least flycatchers, and the next day a gust of titmice and snowbirds filled their places.

The vesper-sparrow, the well-known grass finch, "flies with a quick, sharp movement, showing the two quills in his tail." The junco shows these white quills still more plainly. In the gray morning twilight, when I noticed his return, his ashy form might have passed unnoticed, but for these telltale white stripes.

As the foliage thins, the woodpeckers come more under the observation. The red-headed woodpecker was here yesterday, and to-day the creepers have been circling the crooked apple tree close by the house. The black and white creeper, one of the warbler family, a trifle larger than a wren, was so tame that it only fluttered away when I went toward it, and its barred friend, the true brown-creeper, with strange gait, kept going round and round the trunk, as I followed it, quizzing me with a chirping, "No, you don't." For even the migrant birds become friendly when they are within the protection of the garden close.

The shyest wood bird seems to feel that here the law is set against their destruction. There came and perched during a single day, upon a half-dead, gray-mossed ash, the hairy and downy woodpeckers, much alike in markings, save that the first is larger and has a red head-spot, and the golden-winged woodpecker, who has never left the location where he augured the hole for his nest, but flies about with the heaviness of a pigeon.

Coming and still coming, trooping in by little groups—to catalogue each one would be reviewing New England ornithology. No concerted stampede as yet, save in the case of the swallows. The cedar-birds are again travelling in flocks, and this morning I watched them for almost an hour as they plumed, sitting in rows in the ash tree, where I first saw them in spring, the fierce weather last year having driven them away from December to April. The young have a bunched, home-made look, with their incipient tufts and soft quaker feathers.

October comes in with a day of palpitating heat, like August. Heliotrope blooms in the garden, and Jack roses, who open their carmine lips in wonder, when told by the monk's-hood that it is not June, and that the grasshopper sparrow brought news from the north that the peabody-bird had started. A humming-bird yet darts about the arbour; but be ready, for eastward and northward there are high winds; the sea-smell is sharp in the nostrils, and in spite of the warm yellow light on the pastures, the surf sends a warning note from the shore.

The night was heavy and starless, with frequent gusts of wind, but the storm parted sidewise, and before the late dawn, dull gray clouds with embered edges, like damp wood smouldering, lay in the southeast, and the bird storm the night had brought was spread over dell, garden, and hedge. It had come, the high tide of the fall migration! Many years will pass with nicely graded weather, when the birds slip past unnoticed, and then a storm will bring them on its crest like driftwood.

The Greeks had their Spring Swallow Song; why will not some one give us a bird song of autumn, not pathetic, but tripping with realistic bustle?

Where to look first? Robins were thick on the lawn, wood thrushes scratched under the purple-leaved rose bushes. The berry-tipped dogwood was quaking with the horde that feasted upon it; the foot-paths were alive with the sociable hair-birds, and mingling with them came the beautiful white-throated sparrows.

How many associations follow in the train of a single incident! The white-throated sparrow's soft call is the first bird note that I remember from childhood. In May, returning from a long stay in the city, with my heart swelling with pent-up longing, I stood on the steps of the little station, and as the train ceased breaking the stillness and I could again breathe the earthy fragrance, the first sound was this sparrow's note of welcome. I was sure that his slow call said, "Oh-my! Here-you-are, here-you-are!" and that he was glad that I too had returned, and I wondered vaguely where he had stayed in the interval, and if he had cried as often as I had. In those days, I imagined the birds crept into the cones of the evergreens to spend the winter, and that when the cones snapped open in spring they were released.

The bluebirds hovered for a long time about a Gothic hotel newly erected for them. They peeped into every room, squabbled and fought for apartments as if spring was already urging them to build. Below the garden, the old orchard was on the *qui vive*. The birds had so much to relate to the confiding branches, it mattered little though the trees showed green-netted apples instead of curving buds. One tree, that autumn's storms had stripped of leaves, stretched out a branch set with flowers, and a greedy bud-eating vireo clung to it as if it had bloomed for his sole benefit. All the birds were fearless and hungry, or perhaps their hunger caused their lack of fear. They looked with scorn at the jays, who kept at a distance, for now the eggs, which they had threatened in spring, were sturdy birds capable of self-protection:—

Turn, turn my wheel! All life is brief:
What now is bud will soon be leaf,
    What now is leaf will soon decay;
The wind blows east, the wind blows west;
The blue eggs in the robin's nest
Will soon have wings and beak and breast,
    And flutter and fly away.

Along the lane, the fox-sparrows hop, the olive-backed thrush tried to be bold but failed in courage, and a hermit thrush did not move as I passed. Was he the hermit who enchanted us on May-day, who sang above the smoke of smouldering leaves?

If we only knew it all, knew all that there is to learn between the coming and going! The journey is so short, and before we are thoroughly used to being here, the time has come for our flitting. If only, like the birds, we may keep in our hearts the songs of another season!

The night-hawks, kin of the whip-poor-will, now circle at noon, as in June they did at twilight, and the brown hawk flies toward the sun. Owl notes come nearer at night, for they are leaving the deep woods, and down by the river a stone thrown over the bushes will startle the coveys of black ducks.

One by one the birds will go, until the grackles and vesper-sparrows have vanished and we hear only the notes of a single song-sparrow, and the winter birds quietly take possession.

Under the pointed roof of a summer-house close to the garden, a pair of robins lived all through the ice of last winter. During the day they took shelter in the pines, foraging among the bushes until the berries were picked clean; then they drew nearer to their roost, and finished the season with the fruit of the honeysuckles, climbing around it. Had they eaten this at first, the snow might have besieged and starved them, so they worked outside and left their garrison victualled.

The curtain slowly falls and the troupe of minstrels vanish; the cicadæ have unstrung their fiddles, the glow-worms snuffed their candles, and the swallows that began it all are telling the news in Florida.

The Loom
of Autumn

There she weaves both night and day
A magic web with colours gay.
—Tennyson, "The Lady of Shalott"

Ruined Mill in the Woods near Congress Street

Earth, wedded to the Sun, gave birth to four daughters, and confided the shaping of her vesture to their keeping. Winter, the eldest, silent, ermine-cloaked, wears the northern crown, and from her ice shuttle the pole star rays and gleams. About her, the North Wind roars his gusty love, and by her side Orion watches, as she weaves the snow linen of force-conserving sleep. Spring, the youngest, is the heart flower, with curving pale gold hair bound by the moon's slim crescent, wide curious eyes, like deep frost-free pools that drink the sky, and all her tender body is wrapped in a warm mist, her mother's vital breath. Capriciously she webs a soft green gown, and meshes in its folds snowflakes and violets, and in its trailing length ensnares bright birds, who hold it not imprisonment, and sing so freely that strains of music float from the folds that sweep the ground. The broad girdle to bind the robe about is wrought with gold in dent-de-lion work, and the ruby clasps are gorgets of humming-birds rivetted with diamond raindrops. At her first touch, the mole, deep in his tunnelled home, bestirs himself; the spring breaks forth, and at the cadence of her spinning-song, the motive floats aloft and the swift hawk feels its pang. Even reluctant man, so far withdrawn from Nature, opens his door, and shading his tired eyes, looks for green fields.

Summer has an ampler mien; full-lipped is she, with red-gold hair, crowned with roses, and a generous body. Restful and satisfied she sits in the sun's rays, fanned by her spouse, the South Wind, and weaves the heavy damask robe of matronhood, dense with sweet odours, rich-hued and opulent, such as befits the benignant Earth to wear when, with her arms piled high with ripened sheaves, she gives her children bread.

Autumn, the wayward daughter, steals all her sisters' moods; wedded to the East Wind she scoffs him, and lures the South and the West by turns. She is under spell always to toil to finish the work of others; to shake the nut and mellow apple down, and bear the sweet-skinned grape to the wine-press, but to have no issue of her own. At her touch all growing things blaze with a hectic fire, but their life-blood dries away. And as she chants snatches of broken tunes, that are merely echoes, her voice drops to a cricket's droning, and the silent birds troop off in apprehension. She seems so fair, and yet she wears upon her face Time's ravages; and the gray hollows round the eyes, the treacherous nostril's curve, the too bright lip, all token the ash of passion. With one hand she offers tempting fruits, while the other holds the leash of her messengers—two gaunt hounds, the black frost and the white. She must, for her mother, weave a gorgeous robe for a night's brief revelling, but even as she dyes it bright with every subtle tint the fabric drops away between her hands, leaving them empty.

Autumn passed through the lowlands many days ago, and set her tree-loom by the mill house. All day long she roves afield to fill her shuttle, and weaves all night, so that the fabric shifts and changes with every dawn. When she first came the dodder tied the bushes on the pond's edge in its tangles, and the flame of the cardinal flowers was creeping up the stalks toward its extinguishment. The various goldenrods filled the pastures and tramped cheerfully along the roads, thinning and looking dwarfed as they swarmed in a broken phalanx over the dry hills, then growing stout and ample when they lined the outside of a garden wall, waving gaily over the barrier, and stretching underneath their hungry roots. Surely Midas must have left the underworld some day, and strolled through Yankee lands, brushing the weeds as he passed by with his golden but barren touch.

The Virginia creeper, or five-fingered woodbine, fringed the old grist mill and fell trailing on the ground. Straightway autumn caught at it for her first strand, and everywhere that it grew, around tree trunks in snake-like coils, binding rail fences, clinging to rough briers, it turned crimson, scarlet, yellow, then paled until the leaflets, mesmerized, let go their hold and dropped shrivelling. The maples on the low pond-islands followed the woodbine, but being of much sturdier growth were longer in dying, and for a week or two glowed and flushed, the top leaves fading first, then down, down, down, in the track of the receding life-blood, leaving only the skeleton. The osiers that grow embedded in the water, margining the pond, mixing with the blackened leaves of the pickerel weed, meanwhile have turned into a bank of pink and yellow.

The dogwood, *Cornus florida*, stands out from all the crowding group of trees and bushes, suggesting a moral sketch by Hogarth, which might be called, The Past, Present, and Future of a Virtuous Tree. The gaily coloured leaves are the badges of past service, the rosettes of polished, red, brown-tipped berries make a present feast for worthy pilgrim birds. The well-wrapped flower buds capping the season's growth, with their square parcels, hold the next spring's promise, when by unfurling their white flags they will call a truce with the frost and tell the farmer that he may fearlessly plant his Indian corn.

All this time the South Wind is blowing with summer fervour, only chilled by the lavish dews of earlier twilights. Seeing this, the jealous East Wind starts from the ocean, follows the incoming tide, and rakes heavy salt drift over the marshes, pelting the land with sharp-angled rain, wrestling with the trees until their joints crack, bending the supple to the ground, tearing the stiff and aged limb from limb, beating the striped apples down, mangling the fields of ripened corn with juggernaut wheels, cutting rough channels in the ploughed hillsides, swelling the river until it washes threateningly around the mill house. Autumn, drenched, overpowered, dismayed, her fabric soaked, despoiled, hides until the East Wind has spent his rage. Back creeps the South Wind, keeping well toward the west for shelter, dries the shivering ground, and for a week brings retrospective glimpses.

In the meadows, lately shorn of aftermath, the veins of moisture outline the old growth by fresh green ribbons. Springy roadsides and the banks of quiet streams shelter the purple closed gentian; they are mysterious blossoms, wood-sphinxes, making the silence deeper. Even the bees approach them noiselessly, and lighting on the flower tip give a secret signal for admission. Do forest treasons incubate in those purple caves, and brookside plots and wayside politics, or do the sly bees only step sociably in, to sample an extra brand of honey?

The gentians come almost alone among autumn's tribe of Compositæ; the cardinal lobelia and turtle head are fading when they appear. Back from the shore where the little ridgy hills bound the meadow, and unmown strips teeming with bog-growth guard their treasures, reached by lanes and byways where the great amber-red fox-grape shows its clusters as the browning leaves curl back, where the pepperidge and tulip tree mark the wood-growth, there in the open meadows grows the blue fringed gentian. We may find it by the wayside, or perhaps on a rocky bank where an overflow of earth has washed the seed, but its chosen home is the deep meadow, companioned by brittle ferns, slender Spiranthes, or the white grass of Parnassus. Here in New England, there does not grow at any season a more lovely or individual flower. It brings to September a springtime delicacy, wholly at variance with the autumn's purples, yellows, and scarlets.

It is at best only prophecy to fix set times and seasons for the blooming of wild things, and you may find violets, wild roses, and strawberry flowers, when on a gentian quest. Thoreau, in 1851, records this flower in bloom November 7th, and by a similar chance, Bryant found it even later, among the Cummington hills, though late September, with a week or two for leeway, is its Connecticut season. Its colour pales or deepens according to the quality of soil in which it grows, and with the shade or sunlight of the location. Away from its green surroundings, its perfect blue takes a more purplish tint; but in coming through the twilight of a dense wood-path, into the sudden gold-hazed sunlight of a gentian field, one dreams that the sky, once moulting, dropped its soft-edged feathers on the grass, and earth turned them into flowers.

A jay screams by the river, and at the sound Autumn picks up her web, repairing the threads the wind has torn, but she may not replace them all, for rain has soaked away the freshest hues of her best dyes. The dewberry, trailing down the sandy roadbank, crimsons and bronzes, then brightens near the tip, glowing and paling like splinters of molten steel. The black birch pales, then yellows, until it reaches gold, in company with the rock-maple. The scarlet and pin oaks wear rich enamel, and the black oak is drenched with burgundy. On steep hillsides, the maple-leaved cornel takes a deep raspberry tone, the leaves of the wild roses redden to bronze, and, curling, show bunches of shining red berries, and the eglantine wears her necklace of oval coral beads.

Every bit of earth and rock and sand swarms with Compositæ. The asters range through lilac, violet, purple, white, claiming September as a festival. Their beauty has given them a place in English shrubberies, where they bloom at Michaelmas, when the farmer eats his goose, and they are gathered to trim the churches on the double festival, the purple being called Michaelmas daisies, and the snowy white species,

All Angels. Science has taught us all but what we wish most to learn; has tried to ignore the soul, but burning its fingers in the inextinguishable flame, smarting, smiles a wincing smile and says, "We do not know!" How much poetry we shall miss if the time ever comes when festivals and holidays are no longer kept, but are packed away as the world's childish toys. No fear of it; for all time there will be those who find in simple wayside things—All Angels.

Now again Autumn gathers her thread in armsful. The sassafras is shedding its variegated mittens, and the hickory and walnut their sere yellows; the chestnut leaves are rusty, though the burrs are green; the barberry hangs full of fruit, the purple-berried cornel also; and the white baneberry, the orange-red bitter-sweet, red alder, wintergreen, and creeping partridge vine abound. Berries everywhere, how do they escape the birds? The cautious birds know what will keep the best, and so eat the more substantial food when they can find it. There are yet small, rich seeds, grubs, larvæ, and belated worms, to be preferred to berries. Yellow birds linger where the sunflowers hold their brown-seeded combs; how much nourishment and cold-repelling strength lies in these oily seeds! and why should catbirds and robins eat husky, sour things, while the grape arbour holds a single tempting cluster? Even the jays are not easily driven to acorn dieting.

The last of September! There was a flutter of brown wings this morning, then a halt upon some hemlocks lying toward the south and a flock of birds plume their damp feathers. A glint of white,—so you have returned, merry peabody-birds! we wish all your brother sparrows carried as certain marks of identification as you wear on your white throats. Have you travelled all night? Is there frost and snow in the north? You have returned early! The great crested flycatcher is here, and catbird and other thrushes, and yesterday, by the glint of the sun on a dry twig, a golden-crowned kinglet might be seen.

A flock of plump birds settle where some new grass is seeded, a motley, haphazard group. A glance names them juncos and grasshopper-sparrows. Juncos! the last of a warm September; surely it is very early, and some sharp storm must have warned them. A closer view shows that the birds are all juncos, the males and females, the others being unmoulted young, wearing the stripes of the sparrow tribe.

October comes, and Autumn handles the shuttle more nervously; she has sped here and there for fresh designs, and now in a night weaves in great masses of colour. Yesterday the maples that follow the high river bank all reddened at once; to-day, the nightshade along the fence yellows, and the smooth sumach has an extra coat of varnish. A noise, like the croaking of tree toads, comes from the nuthatches that are skirting the branches and trunks of trees; the pond frogs are silent, and the hylodes of the spring "peep" now and then, having exchanged the marsh for tree dwellings. The cricket chirps day and night, and at twilight some teal-ducks fly over on their way to salt water, as rapidly as swallows, but so low that the glistening of their green feathers can be seen.

No frost, but Autumn roving, steps over the wall into the garden; before this she has only looked over. The scarlet sage blazes indignantly, the quilled Dahlias bob their prim heads and nod in grave apprehension to the hedge of nasturtiums. The favoured chrysanthemums smile and look knowing, for they are already potted and sure of protection. Low-lying mats of verbenas glow with comfort, and the carnations and more rugged roses pass the word to stray pansies: "Never fear; winter only can alarm us." The honeysuckle blooms unconcerned, a pear tree holds fresh sprouts and a spray of blossoms, and as if mating this freak in the animal world, two humming-birds pause to rest on the trellis. Where are they from? Their flocks passed away in the middle of September. Have they lost their almanac, and do they think aphides and honey will hold out through their long journey?

The kingfishers and blue herons are about, and the larks are stalking through the beach meadows. In crossing a rough hillside, covered by dwarf sumachs and briers, a brown thrush unearthed, in scratching, some of the leathery shells of the eggs of the black snake. He pecked at them unconsciously, not dreaming that from them had emerged a tribe of his chief enemies.

Now comes the second reign of the orchard. In May she queened it with flowers, and now again with her buxom fruit. Beauty is deeply bedded in the apple's skin; look at its texture, grain, and harmonious colouring. This russet with greenish cast, sucked by a fly, might yield a book-binder hints for the cover of some quaint Walton. The Baldwin, as fervid red levant morocco, in untempered Jansen style, should wrap Laus Veneris. This stippled pippin could guard Gerarde's Herball, and these generous greenings, wrought in gold, with angle, curve, and floriature, might fitly bear the genial stamp of Grolier, while Cobden-

Sanderson could ask for no daintier pattern for his tooling than the gold leaf-shadows dancing and latticing the heaps of the Northern Spy.

The apple holds the first place in the pictorial farm pageant, even though the giant mangles, like lumps of beef, pile up the wagons, and onions, carrots, and turnips yield greater profit. The pumpkin still exists and grins among the cornstalks, but the apple, though pursued by moth and rust, is yet the bright, crisp fruit our forbears deemed it, and every autumn sees its panorama. The apples are picked and sorted into heaps, and the surplus being shaken down, the ox carts crawl with them to the cider-mill. With what a crunch the teeth meet in the fruit, when exercise and the keen air make the blood tingle and parch the throat, and what a pleasure lies in the quick gush of the responsive juice! The apple is the friend of every one.

The cider-mill, on one side half fallen down, and patched with rough chestnut boards, hangs over the tumbling stream and, being idle all the year, save for a month or two, vines have crawled over it and mosses spread their mimic forests on the roof. The other portion, bare and new, serves as post-office and the village store. The stream leaps down and swings the wheel around, the millstones crush, and the apples spurt, then cake to pumice between the layers of straw, and bees swarm thick about the mass, and no one hurries. The oxen chew their cud, the men who grind the apples move lazily, or sit and chew straws, while the passer-by may help himself at will to straw, or cloudy cider from a battered cup. Some boys, with chilled red legs and trousers high rolled, are bobbing barrels in a pool to rinse and swell them.

An odour of fields, orchards, woods, sweeps past, joined to the yeasty smell of fermentation. The amber fluid as yet feels no pulsing in its veins, and merely cloys the stomach; but give it time and it will turn the drinker's temper and fog his brain quicker than all the wiles of Veuve Cliquot. The sugar-maple drops its leaves with a staccato sound, and the stream and wind and bees intone a part song, the last verse of the orchard melody that they began in May. Drink a health to autumn, a health to all seasons, to all weathers, if we may but keep our hearts young and remember our Earth-mother!

A few John o' Dreams days, no signs, no forebodings, then the steel-white sky looks forbidding. Warm noon cools suddenly; no wind, a hush over the lowlands and up creeps a dense, tangible coldness. By the mill house, the green malarial mist rises from the dead vegetation, soaking and melting away in the pond, where no current washes the margin. Autumn's shuttle falls from between her numbing fingers, and the loomed cloth sleeves, as she slips the leash of the white frost hound and he glides through the meadows. All night he runs, breathing on the weeds as he passes, trampling the grass, touching the mossy stones and the tree bark, his breath remaining in white crystals. He comes up and slips through the garden, but his force is spent, and he only sniffs at the heliotropes and stiff edgings of coleus, and crushes the rank marrow vines. At dawn the hoar lies thick, dandelion rosettes gleam in the sunlight, and the leaves ripen and scatter.

After the first frost a golden lapse follows, a pensive time between sleeping and waking. Nature is ripe, deadly ripe, and Autumn pauses thrilled, hardly daring to breathe lest the enchanted fabric should vanish, yet half believing the robe is something more than a bright phantom. Then there comes a pantomime, a ballet interlude before the last act. Beauty gathers, the seasons seem topsy-turvy, the earth is saturated with colour, and the gay birds of summer in sober dominos, silent as becomes their part, pervade their former haunts. The brown water holds argosies of leaf boats, and other leaves, tricked out in flower colours, dance on the grass, while katydids and crickets twang their little banjos, and the pines wave applause. What dainty disguises the wood things wear! The medeola, with whorled, two-storied stalk, is dressed in buff and pink, with blue berries for a top knot, each stalk a unique thing. False buckwheat covers the fence rails with its seeds, reclothes the mullein stalks, luring one to think it a new flower, and many berries mingle their colours with the yellowing ferns.

The hedges now are at their best. We have no trim thorn hedgerows, leashed by ivy and "lush woodbine"; ours are the patient growths that follow old walls, claiming the rough stone's protection from the stubble scythe. Out of ploughed fields step back the sumachs, the fragrant clethra, meadow-sweet, shad-bush, white thorn, cornel, dwarf willow, flowering raspberry and wild rose. Up from the roadside climb bayberry, sunflowers, elecampane, and hazels hang their fringed-podded nuts, all clasping hands to make New England's waysides the fascinating things they are. And how we love these hedges! They yield surprises, from pussy-willow time until the snow, and even then above it the witch-hazel waves its boughs. The autumn hedges are the colour-bearers for the sombre fields, and as the wind puffs, birds and leaves whirl aloft.

Middle October comes, and all along the road bouncing-Bet is laughing, blue flax blooms in stone crannies, and toad-flax spreads in the gravel banks; iron-weed, yarrow, clover, ox-eye daisies, are fresh as in hay-days, and moth-mullein thrives in every waste. Chestnut burrs relax from very ripeness, and cast their freight upon wood-sorrel, and burr-marigolds blaze in the same places that the marsh-marigolds gilded. Fall wheat is two inches high and strawberries are in flower; cider is flowing, and there are flower patches on hillside apple trees.

Nature lets loose her fancy to show what she can do, setting at naught man's wisdom, and mocking his forecasts and his calendars.

When October comes, the farmer promptly takes out his air-tight stove and plants it in his sitting-room, putting therein a fire of coals to stifle out what life remains in him after the summer toil. When early twilights, more than the cold, draw the household around its hearth-heart, the logs piece out the scant day with their treasured surplus of sunlight. Nature draws out and gratifies each sense with colour, per-fume, heat, and all the while the wood juices whistle a little tune, learned long ago in sapling days, from the peeping marsh frogs. When pine cones add their incense to the flames, with it returns the forest perfume, and if we close the eyes, the thoughts go springward to pink-pouched cypripedes and hermit thrushes.

A few more golden days and now once again the wind returns; low puffs, sharp moaning from the east, then northern gusts. October has but two more days to live. Will the wind drop to-night? No! blow, rack, blow, the stars glisten as if a veil had been torn away between them and the earth.

Another day: the wind veers from north to west and lessens; to-night will bring a "killing frost." The gardener draws the sashes on the violet frames, covers the plant pit tightly with straw mats, and muffles a few pet border things to give them a last chance. The farmer's wife takes in her geraniums, slipped in old tin cans, her amaryllis from the south porch, her cacti and Fuchsias, putting them in the warmest window of the kitchen, takes from the shed the apples spread for drying, and tomatoes kept for seed, and tucks an old quilt about her ragged chrysanthemums.

Four o'clock and the wind dies away, but leaves all its sharpness in the air. How clear it is! You can trace all the distant hills, the ripples on the waters of the Sound clearly mark the currents, and the Long Island shore, twelve miles across, is sharply definite. Every twig snap resounds, and the jay's scream is percussive. Ah! they are nutting now, carrying the acorns from the red oaks in the dell to a hollow sassafras, and the squirrels chuckle and look very wise. The air is alert with a sense of change. You are restless also, you cannot go indoors, the garden of summer hours holds out its begging hands, already cold and bloodless.

To sleep, dear flowers, go to sleep; your light must be blown out, but your work is well done. Many messages you have carried from the garden in your persuasive language, many frail humming-birds your hearts have held and nourished, and you have drawn sunshine earthward to the sorrowful. Children have kissed you, and you have filled lonely hearts with bright memories. And you, dear roses, you have veiled a silent breast in its earth sleep and your fragrance followed the spirit through the morning gates. By root and bulb and seed, your forms are all perpetuate.

Lie low, nasturtiums, release your grasp, even your sharp tongues will not save you. Carnations, your courage only prolongs a useless struggle. Convolvuli, your cups were made for sweet dew-wine, sherbet will break them.

You alone, faithful honeysuckles that wall the garden, have yet a lease. When your vanilla-scented flowers vanish, your thick persistent leaves and firm berries will shelter and feed the winter birds. We will call you the garden's Royal Inn; what bird have you not harboured cheerfully, how many little claws have signed your register? Transients and steady lodgers, prolific wrens that brought out three broods of a season, robins that only stopped to see how the strawberries and currants ripened, the oriole who paused to fray a string, that bound you once, that he might lash his sky boat, and at evening the vesper-sparrow came, and facing the glowing west poured out his heart in song; and still your hospitable thatch will shelter all that ask, until fresh buds bring renewal. Wide beds of bloom, you are already changing; your sap has ebbed. Nature, unhampered, never deals to death with a painful, stinging blow. The bird that the hawk grasps feels no pain; the pang is deadened by a purposeful mesmeric power.

Softly! the change is coming! In the southwest the sky is a clear red, fading through gold to a blue white. The moon, many hours high, gives a gradual icy light, and the clear air is stinging. What is Autumn doing down by the mill house? She is haggard and cold, her weaving is falling away and her shuttle is warping as with trembling fingers she frees the leash from the black frost hound, her executioner. Away! river, wall, trellis, nothing impedes his blasting course!

A pall lies on the ground the first morning after, but the next brings frost flowers, which graft their fairy blossoms upon the heliotropes. The frozen sap between the bark and stem, expanded by the sun, turning into crystals the second night, curving in the thread-like shapes of its former channels, covers the plants with gypsum flowers.

The spell is breaking, Autumn's garish robe frays and tears, and, floating away, a fragment catches here and there, colouring the sere fields. Then the East Wind whirls his trembling mate up through the webless loom, mocking its emptiness, and a gypsy child, gathering fagots, binds the warped shuttle in her pack. The miller rakes away the huddling dead leaves, lest they should choke the flume, and, heaping high, sets them ablaze. The imprisoned gases mingle their opalescence with the smoke, and through the flame appears the year's mirage that we call Indian Summer.

A Winter Mood

Here might I pause and bend in reverence
To Nature and the power of human mind.
—WORDSWORTH, *The Prelude*

White Pines on Oldfield Road and Pine Creek

Blow all the day, gray wind, blow all the day! Sweep the cold sky and polish its jewels, sweep all the earth's corners and release their vapours. Blow all the day, gray wind, and bury the wood-path in brown leaves; pluck even the leaf rags from the tenacious beeches, as the crow rends the last shred from a carcass.

Whirl in the mottled sands, and cover the bronze seaweeds, the gold and silver shells, bits of wreckage bright with barnacles, the drift fagots, the tracks of the wader, and the ridged sound waves, left by the beating of the ebbing ocean. Call to the sand reeds: their slender pipes have grown shrill and they whistle an answer; they are hoarse, their fluting is over.

Beat on the marshes; the tawny grass flattens and does not rise behind you. Puff through the lane and salt meadows—at last you have raised evil spirits; the ghosts of burr-marigolds, of avens, tick-trefoil, and goose-grass, like brocken witches, rise, and following in your wake, fasten hooked claws to the hide of the cattle, burrowing deep in their rough coats, and flying aloft on winged broomsticks, make a tour of perpetuation. Brush heaps are smouldering by the fields' edges; circle about, then, gray wind, until the flame devours them. Labour all day, gray wind, but when the sun goes down, cloud-curtained, cease, and bid the wild sheep that graze in northern pastures, drop their crystal fleece to wrap the earth from winter.

A morning in winter; can there be morning in the dead season? There is no dead season. Men say that it is summer, or autumn, or winter, but Nature has set no fixed bounds to her actions, and does not perish when she casts off her apparel, but, gathering her forces to herself, prepares for new effort. Nature knows but two changes, putting forth and withdrawing, and between these there is a constant transition. We call the first of them birth, the last, death, and choose to surround them with mystery. Nature, left to herself, has gentle gradations, blending all from the first breath to the last, as she mingles the prismatic colours, with no gap to measure where youth ends or age begins. We fasten attributes to things, and hold them there by mere persistency. There is no really dead season; there are no snows so deep but somewhere in the firs the crossbill holds his sign of the sacred legend, no ice so thick but under it the warm current stirs, no age so dreary that love may not quicken it until eternal spring.

The first snow fell in the night, not deeply, but tenderly, shielding the newly bared things from the grasp of the ice. It came flake upon flake, clinging, not driving pitiless; beginning softly and ending as the late sun pushed through the clouds, and yawned, uncertain whether to rise or to take one more nap, letting his pale hair straggle on the cloud pillows; then succumbing, wrapped the mist once more about him.

What silence! the cold has chained even the waves of sound, and the new snow muffles the echoes. Open the frost-engraved window; the air enters in half-vapourized particles, cutting the throat and nostrils like diamond dust. Yellow light covers the snow, not sunlight nor light from the sun's direction, but a weighed-down refraction; the solid brown sky shades to buff toward the eastward, the landscape perspective is altered, and there are no shadows. The sociable, nestling snow has no depth and thaws at a breath, yet it is a magician, writing cheerful winter on everything, and it is the fitting interpreter for the season of silence, when Nature's voice is hushed and she is less responsive.

There comes a faint, lisping chirp, and a flock of white-vested juncos wheel from the arbour. Many hopes of food and shelter for birds surround a dwelling whose deep porches are hung with evergreen honeysuckle, with a garden arbour or two, and a copse of pine, fir, and hemlocks, or hedges of arbor-vitæ, the true life trees. When snow and frost bury all other sources of food, then do not forget to scatter a handful of buckwheat, oats, or crumbs to the pensioners. How inexpressibly dear are these lodgers that we shelter; they keep the eye keen and the heart warm in the waiting. The titmice are fearless, and come within hand-reach as they pry in and out or play hide-and-seek about the knot holes with the pine finch and nuthatch; they are very sociable and court rather than reject human society.

Come out, then, under the sky. The north wind has made rifts in the clouds and the sun comes and goes at pleasure. The snow has dropped from the firs and now only lightens their shadows, and on the ground acts as a tablet of wax to receive the etched impressions of the trees; sharp grass blades pierce through the depressions and little thaw pools outline the foot-path. On a day like this, forms are unmuffled and the lines are clear cut. The trees show all their muscles and sinews, and the rocks, brightly stained by lichens, peer between their grim boles. Now the reign of the evergreens—trees, ferns, and mosses— triumphantly begins. The Christmas tree by the hearth centres the heart-beats of winter, and its mates in the copse take out of doors the same Christmas feeling, and spreading their loving arms draw the brave little birds to shelter, and, to satisfy their hunger, dangle before them well-thatched cone-granaries.

In groups and lines straggling to the meadow are pines, spruces, and firs. In the wild fields the cedars, looking so black in the distance, grow warm-hued on nearer acquaintance, and on the ground the juniper bushes seem like the nests of the obsolete dodo.

Black and white winter, are you both flowerless and songless? It may seem so, but there is both music and colour; for the tones of winter are as really distinctive as those of all other seasons. If you search, as you have done each day, in the spring, summer, or autumn, you will find constantly a new beauty, a fresh surprise. For birds, you may see here-abouts, upwards of thirty species between late November and early March; not all in one day, or one month even, but scattered according to food and to changes of temperature. The juncos and snowflakes, birds of the most rigorous weather, owls small and large, hen hawks, crows, jays, and shrikes. Robins, bluebirds, and song-sparrows are kept with us by genial weather, as well as the purple finches, crossbills, siskins, nuthatches, titmice, winter-wrens, the golden-crowned kinglet, and the edge of the woodpecker tribe. In the salt meadows you may see the field and shore larks, wild ducks and geese, and in the stubble the quail, and perhaps a few wild pigeons in the thin woods.

Let us go up the road to the lane that winds round the hill until it, by twisting, caps it—the lane where the wild apples bloomed in May. The first impression is of sombreness. The thin snow carpets the road to the stone wall, but through it break sprays of the smoky-seeded goldenrod, and the skeleton nests of wild carrot, while by the gate a barberry bush glows with coral, and upon this gate some quail are perching. Surely here is colour enough. The birds walk away uncon-cernedly, with long strides, like warmly coated little boys who tramp in the snow for amusement. The road cuts through a trap-crest, and the deep blue stone, stained and streaked with rusty brown where it faces the weather, adds one more tint to the palet. In the field on the left are the telltale tracks of wild rabbits—hop, sit! hop, sit! The trail runs through the bushes and under the fence; there they are making a feast of cast-away turnips.

The split, empty milkweed pods point upward with their sharp fingers, and the black-purple berries shine on the polished green strands of cat-brier. It seems more like a metal than anything organic and living, as it grasps your clothing tightly and winds you into its clutches. I think this vine must have been the model for the treacherous barbed-wire fencing, and its hooks are often the meat-safe where the butcher-bird hangs his provisions. No wonder that the chat feels secure from nest-hunters when he builds in a cat-brier tangle.

Beyond is a crimson patch of sumach berries, with their steeple-shaped bunches, and the bitter-sweet hangs its red quartered fruit nigh in the top of a cedar. Something is fluttering there, pulling and pecking at the berries; soon the black, polished beak and cinnamon crest of the cedar-bird emerges and the vibrations of the dense green branches indicate others. Winter birds seldom go far from houses in their haunts or habits of feeding, but seem to say quiescently: "We are but few; let us huddle together. If the snow hides our food, we will go near to man's dwellings, and he will see that we are fed and protected. He may, perhaps, shoot a great owl, or the hawk, and the marsh duck, but he will seldom hurt us, for we are the King's minstrels. So we love man, for without him, his houses, gardens, and orchards, to shield us, the hawk and the shrike would prevail over us, and in the forests we never dare to warble as freely as we do in the hedges."

The narrowing lane is quite birdless, in spite of the red-berried alders and the thistles, that have not all scattered their winged seeds, and the ghostly sprays of the asters. The wild rose stalks glow red, as if new blood was already flowing, and the raspberry canes are pink with a pearly bloom. Through the tangles of underbrush the white mottled trunks of the silver birch pole their way, and the cupped seed-pods of the tulip tree give a dice-like rattle in the wind. Look forward and back at the thick woods of chestnut, and the oaks with gray trunks, stretching in the distance. The orchard twists iron-black branches where the jays jeer, as they quarry the frozen apples. The lane runnel is skimmed by a crust of ice, which is broken and jagged in places, and across it lies a chestnut, felled years ago and abandoned as worthless until, nibbled by fungi and lichens, it is slowly resolving into earth particles. In the border of the swamp the long cat-tail flags, gone to seed, wave wool-white, as if the missing tails of Bo Peep's flock were awaiting their owners.

Under the path the runnel drops and flows over the stones; the green weeds on the bottom sway as they do at midsummer. Dip your hand in the water; it warms more than chills you. Underneath the bushes the ground-pine is spicy, and the thrifty club mosses make miniature forests. The frailer ferns have vanished, but the hardy aspleniums, aspidiums, and the rock polypody still keep their fronds, and the mosses, with their seed-vessels held like fixed bayonets, swarm in armies and flourish where the surface is grassless. Mats of Sphagnum cover the bog, and cupped lichens fill in the cracks of the rocks and gnarled trees.

Stop! here by the wall, in a sun-streak, the witch-hazel shows its gold threads; pause as you pass, and listen to its story of the winter-opening flower, of youth in old age.

Zigzag goes the lane to the top of the hill; a pasture, whose bars were left down, when in November the last cow walked through, holds an old chestnut, and from it a flock of crows have just flown. In the next field, which marks the edge of a clearing, the cornstalks are stacked like the tents of an Indian village, and the field mice rustle in and out among them, the crows keeping a jealous watch. On the edge of the farm-house piazza some fowl are roosting, and give a life touch with their red combs and gray and white feathers. How welcome seems the smoke that floats from the stone chimney, and how pleasant is the greeting that comes from the geraniums inside the window, who turn their blooms to the glass as if they tried to keep count of the passers. The bark of the ragged brown collie sounds cheerfully human; he curves his back and wags his tail in a most apologetic manner, as if to say, "I must bark for my living, but you know that I am really quite glad to see you."

This is home, the hand-mark of man close on the edge of the woods. At night, a light from the window will traverse the darkness, breaking and dispersing it, as the eye of the Maker beamed through the void. With the dwelling we find the birds again. The snowflake, whose soft coat is white, with the brown leaf stains of autumn; the Canada nuthatch walks, head down, round a plane tree, and a winter-wren peeps out from the woodpile. For a little while the sun again overcomes the clouds, and you can hear the soft drip of the snow thawing on the fences, and the "day, day, day," of the titmouse makes music. One more turn and we gain the hill-top; we are above the world and surrounded by picturesque winter. The water of the Sound is gray-blue, but with the changing flaws it wears as many hues as the moods of the stirring winds. Not a sail is to be seen nor even a smoke puff. Two lighthouses stand at the reef-points, the tide creeps over the sand beach in a crescent. By the mouth of the creek, the bells of St. Mary's hang silent, the gulls sweep about and float on the water, and clattering, flock on the long sand bars. Next lies the village, with its various houses nestled among the bare elms, a rampart of outlines. To the eastward stand tall chimneys that breathe flame and cinders, a factory city, whose thin, piercing spires are partly hidden by smoke.

Look at these chimneys also, though they break the harmonious circle, we must wear clothes and we must eat, for we may not all find sweetness in white oak acorns, like Thoreau. In winter, which lays bare the earth, man's needs appear, and intensify his personal limitations. Mutual dependence, and not isolation, was the plan of creation. Man needs the earth, and the earth needs man's stamp of progression.

From the village, the hill rolls upward to our feet, and parting and meeting again the hills sweep on until they are shut off by the sky cover. Farms near at hand, farms on the slopes, farms standing boldly against the horizon, and over all the white wings of the dove of peace are folded.

At last the sun fiercely breaks the clouds and drops to a majestic setting. There is no winter, if you can view it from this point, only the splendour of a tense concentration, of a power beyond the present. The snow grows purple, the clouds dive down the horizon, the sun, in the southwest, has now reached its solstitial turning.

Is winter the end or a clearer beginning? The wind goes abroad and drives the sound of the surf into the pine tops, the blue jays have vanished. The owl still keeps in his cover, but the titmouse creeps closer and nods gaily. Can this crystalline transformation be the year in its dotage, a vague second childhood? Age and winter should take for their sign the witch-hazel, the flower of unconquered hope. There is no winter or age for the heart that feels Nature's throbbings, and crowns the earth's beauty with human brotherhood. White-haired frost is not decay's grim-visaged servant, but a transmuter, wearing invisible on its breast the circle sign of the whole plan.

Our Dr. Holmes, a little past his seventieth birthday, wrote in a letter thus: "It is a mixed kind of feeling with which one reaches the top of this Pisgah and peeps over into the mists that hover over Jordan. I felt as if Bryant was old and out of sight on his seventieth birthday, but now—bless me! why, what did the Psalmist mean with his 'threescore years and ten'? Think of Tennyson, of Gladstone, of Disraeli, of the stout old fellows who ride to the hounds in England—of old Radetsky—and the possibilities—think of THOMAS PARR! Think of Henry Jenkins! That is the way one feels and talks to himself when he finds himself driven into that fast-narrowing corner, where the drivers—the deaf, inexorable years—have at last edged us almost without our knowing they were driven. The horizon flies as we travel westward, the sun goes back as it did for Joshua. At fifty years seventy seemed like sunset. At seventy, we find it is as yet only cheerful, shining afternoon. Nature has more artifices than all the human conjurers that ever lived." This is the witch-hazel spirit, the talisman for the twilight of year or years.

The shadows grow more purple, twigs snap, and ice-strands web the thaw pools. The distant water blackens and swallows the flashes from the beacon. Smoking clouds linger above the sunset; then night gathers her garments close. But the titmouse, retreating to his hole, still declares that it is "day! day! day!"

Notes

INTRODUCTION

1   "one Connecticut editorialist": "Mabel Osgood Wright," *Bridgeport Post*, n.d., n.p. (Mabel Osgood Wright [MOW] Clippings File, Bridgeport Public Library [BPL]).

"As another writer noted": "Novelist Dies in Fairfield," *Bridgeport Post*, 17 July 1934, n.p. (MOW Vertical File, Fairfield Historical Society [FHS]).

"the 'back-to-nature' movement": See Peter J. Schmitt, *Back to Nature: The Arcadian Myth in Urban America* (New York: Oxford Univ. Press, 1969).

"As Wright observed": MOW, "Life Outdoors and Its Effect upon Literature," *Critic* 42 (1903): 310. In 1899, Wright wrote that "the great desire of thinking people for a broader life in nature . . . is one of the most healthful and hopeful features at the close of this century" (*Bird-Lore* 1 [1899]: 29).

2   "the naturalist E. O. Wilson": See Edward O. Wilson, *The Diversity of Life* (Cambridge, Mass.: Harvard Univ. Press, 1992).

" 'I am very glad,' wrote Wright": MOW, "After Legal Protection, What?" *Bird-Lore* 4 (1902): 72.

3   "Samuel Osgood": For more on Osgood and his achievements, see Annie Russell Marble, "Mabel Osgood Wright—A Lover of Birds," *Boston Evening Transcript*, 11 December 1926, n.p. (MOW Vertical File, FHS); James Osborne Wright, "Rev. Samuel Osgood, S.T.D., LL.D.," *New England Historical and Genealogical Register* 36 (1882): 113–22; Obituary of Samuel Osgood, *Magazine of American History* 5 (1880): 399–400; Obituary of Samuel Osgood, *New York Genealogical and Biographical Record* 12 (1881): 148; D. Hamilton Hurd, ed., *History of Fairfield County, Connecticut*, vol. 1 (Philadelphia: J. W. Lewis and Co., 1881), 332.

"a three-story, brick house": MOW, *My New York* (New York: Macmillan, 1926), 19–20.

4   "Mosswood, an eighteen-room house": After 1869, Osgood changed the name of the estate to Waldstein, combining the German words *wald* (meaning "woods" or "forest") and *stein* (meaning "stone"). Anti-German sentiment at the beginning of World War I led the family to change the name back to *Mosswood* (MOW, *My New York*, 20).

"property was said to have been": Hurd, 331.

"a showpiece of contemporary cottage design": One Fairfield resident remembers that "Mabel had a good sense of humor and when asked what style of architecture the house was she remarked it was Queen Anne in front and Mary Ann behind" (Mary Sturges Frier, "Reminiscence of Mary Sturges Frier," Typescript [FHS]).

"Andrew Jackson Downing": For more on Downing, see David Schuyler, *Apostle of Taste: Andrew Jackson Downing, 1815–1852* (Baltimore: Johns Hopkins Univ. Press, 1996); Adam Sweeting, *Reading Houses and Building Books: Andrew Jackson Downing and the Architecture of Popular Antebellum Literature, 1835–1855* (Hanover, N.H.: Univ. Press of New England, 1996); and George B. Tatum and Elisabeth Blair MacDougall, eds., *Prophet with Honor: The Career of Andrew Jackson Downing, 1815–1852* (Washington, D.C.: Dumbarton Oaks, 1989).

"Osgood created extensive gardens": "Fairfield Country Day School, in Beautiful Historic Setting, Shuns 'Theories', Stresses Time-Tested Fundamentals in Teaching," *Bridgeport Sunday Post*, 6 April 1941, n.p. (MOW Clippings File, BPL).

"According to one account": Hurd, 331.

"Many of these rocks were carved": The poets so immortalized included Emerson, Longfellow, Bryant, Chaucer, Tasso, Dante, Alfieri, Petrarch, Shakespeare, Goethe, Schiller, Corneille, Milton, Wordsworth, Keble, Scott, Homer, and Virgil (Hurd, 331).

"this wooden pulpit": Though the tower is now gone, the inscription "God and Our Country 1862" is still visible on "Pulpit Rock."

"Osgood changed the name of the street": Arthur H. Hughes and Morse S. Allen, *Connecticut Place Names* (Hartford: Connecticut Historical Society, 1976), 171; "Fairfield Estate with Big History Soon to Be Sold," *New York Times*, 13 October 1913, n.p. (MOW Clippings File, FHS).

"Mabel Gray was born": Osgood had two other daughters, Agnes Haswell and Bertha Stevens.

5   "she once told an interviewer": "Visit to Famous Garden of Past Discloses Shrine Dedicated to Many Poets," n.s., n.d., n.p. (MOW Clippings File, FHS).

"In a revealing aside": Marble. See also "Passing of Mabel Osgood Wright, Noted Novelist and Naturalist, Recalls Highlights of Her Splendid Life," *Bridgeport Sunday Post*, 22 July 1934, n.p. (CAS Records, BMS).

"his essay 'The Education of Daughters'": Samuel Osgood, *The Hearth-Stone: Thoughts upon Home-Life in Our Cities*, rev. ed. (New York: E. P. Dutton, 1876), 228.

"good training would produce a daughter": Osgood, *Hearth-Stone*, 225.

"James Osborne Wright": Most of James Wright's publications are bibliographies and catalogs of private collections, but he also edited a collection of the poems of John Ruskin (New York: Merrill and Baker, 1880). His book shop was located at 6 East 42nd Street in Manhattan.

"In her autobiography": MOW, *My New York*, 224–25.

"she notes elsewhere": "Mabel Osgood Wright Recalls Pleasures of a Busy Literary Life," *Bridgeport Sunday Post*, 8 March 1925, n.p. (MOW Clippings File, FHS).

"After a period of travel in Europe": During her European travels, Wright published a series of letters from abroad in the *Bridgeport Standard* that, apart from some poetry published in the *New York Evening Post* (with the aid of William Cullen Bryant), constitutes her first published work (Marble).

6   "one journalist noted": Marble. In *The Garden of a Commuter's Wife* (New York: Macmillan, 1903), Wright offered a fictionalized version of her European journey: "One year was spent in travel, the other in a quiet English country home, these two years being divided by an illness of the kind where through sheer weakness one loses gravity, and seems to float through space seeking a footing either in heaven or earth and finding neither" (17).

"Wright once told an interviewer": "Mabel Osgood Wright Recalls Pleasures."

"In 1925 she recounted": "Mabel Osgood Wright Recalls Pleasures."

"Edmund Clarence Stedman": In a 17 October 1893 letter, Stedman was more cautious than Wright suggests: "I read your 'May Day' when it appeared, & thought it charming, & ought to have guessed that you wrote it. The others are lovely prose idylls of nature. When the question comes as to making a book of such pieces, I can say at once that, at this period and among the multitude of books, I doubt whether the sale would be remunerative. People are changing from interest in nature to a longing for dramatic life & feeling. . . . Of course a book exquisitely got-up, like Ellwanger's Garden's Story & devoted to nature-studies as exquisite as yours, would do well if issued by a laudable publisher" (MOW Autograph Album, Fairfield Public Library [FPL]). Stedman refers to George H. Ellwanger, *The Garden's Story; or, Pleasures and Trials of an Amateur Gardener* (New York: D. Appleton and Co., 1889). After reading the entire book in manuscript, Stedman grew more enthusiastic, telling Wright on 16 April 1894 that "anyone who cares for outdoor life" would buy her book (MOW Autograph Album). See also his 15 May 1894 letter (MOW Autograph Album).

"George P. Brett": George P. Brett moved to Darien, Connecticut, in 1891, and to Greenfield Hill in Fairfield in 1903. James Wright submitted the book to Brett on 3 February 1894, without mentioning that his wife was the author. On 21 February, Brett replied to James Wright, requesting a meeting with the author. Two days later, Brett spoke to Mabel and suggested that the book be revised and resubmitted. On 2 April, Brett conveyed the substance of a reader's report, which recommended changing some words, standardizing the botanical names, omitting some poems and an entire chapter ("By the River"), and asking Wright to double-check some factual information. Apparently, Wright made the requested changes (Macmillan Company Records, Brett Letterbooks, Manuscripts and Archives Division, New York Public Library, Astor, Lenox, and Tilden Foundations [NYPL]).

"They appeared in April, 1894": Wright's memory fails her only slightly. *The Friendship of Nature* was first published on 15 May 1894. It was reprinted in June and July 1894; in May, August, and October 1895; in July 1898; and in a new edition in September 1906. The book originally appeared in two editions, in a smaller duodecimo size and a larger "large paper" edition limited to 250 copies. An unbound preview copy of the book is located at the CAS Burr Street Office.

"British and American critics": See the *Dial* 17 (16 Sept. 1894): 159; *New York Times*, 28 May 1894, 3. Holmes's letter is quoted in Marble's article and appears in MOW's Autograph Album (FPL). The *Philadelphia Evening Bulletin* is quoted in MOW, *Birdcraft* (New York: Macmillan, 1895), 319.

7   "the other women writers": The letters appear in MOW's Autograph Album (FPL). Spofford refers to Alphonse Karr, *A Tour round My Garden*, ed. J. G. Wood (New York: Routledge, 1855).

"the works of other writers": See Katherine M. Abbott, *Trolley Trips: The Historic New England Coast* (Lowell, Mass.: K. M. Abbott, 1899); Frank Samuel Child, *An Old New England Town* (New York: Scribner, 1895) and other works; Alice Morse Earl, *Old Time Gardens Newly Set*

Forth (New York: Macmillan, 1901); and Lena May McCauley, *The Joy of Gardens* (Chicago: Rand McNally, 1911).

"One contemporary described her": "Mabel Osgood Wright Recalls Pleasures." By eliminating the need for portable darkrooms, the dry plate process transformed photography into a pursuit suitable for even the novice picture-taker.

8   "her father could in 1877 proclaim": Samuel Osgood, *Mile Stones in Our Life-Journey*, rev. ed. (New York: E. P. Dutton, 1877), 315.

"a busy suburb of nearby Bridgeport": For more on suburbanization in Connecticut, see Kenneth T. Jackson, *Crabgrass Frontier: The Suburbanization of the United States* (New York: Oxford Univ. Press, 1985); John R. Stilgoe, *Borderland: Origins of the American Suburb, 1820-1939* (New Haven: Yale Univ. Press, 1988); and Nathan Laselle Whetten, *Studies of Suburbanization in Connecticut* (1936-39; New York: Arno, 1974).

"'colonial revival' photos": Madelyn Kay Moeller, "Ladies of Leisure: Domestic Photography in the Nineteenth Century" (M.A. thesis, University of Delaware, May 1989), 126. For additional context, see Frances Benjamin Johnston, "What a Woman Can Do with a Camera," *Ladies Home Journal*, September 1887, 6-7. On Nutting, see his *Connecticut Beautiful* (Framingham, Mass.: Old America Company, 1923). See also John R. Stilgoe, "Popular Photography, Scenery Values, and Visual Assessment," *Landscape Journal* 3 (1984): 111-22. For more on the colonial revival in Connecticut, see William Butler, "Another City upon a Hill: Litchfield, Connecticut, and the Colonial Revival," *The Colonial Revival in America*, ed. Alan Axelrod (New York: Norton, 1985), 15-51.

"as Wright observed in the *Critic*": MOW, "Life Outdoors," 310. Wright expressed similar sentiments in an article she wrote for the *Fairfield News*, noting that "in those days the way of the beginner was tortuous in the extreme" because of "the lack of popular books upon birds at reasonable prices, that could teach the identification of birds and non-technical histories of their lives.... The only books available to me in my youth were a weighty and not very accurate volume by Samuels and a four volume pocket edition of Wilson and Bonapartes Ornithology published in 1831" ("Conn. Audubon Society Holds Annual Meet," *Fairfield News*, 9 June 1923, 5). Wright refers to Edward A. Samuels, *Among the Birds: A Series of Sketches for Young Folks, Illustrating the Domestic Life of Our Feathered Friends* (Boston: Nichols and Noyes, 1868); and Alexander Wilson and Charles Lucian Bonaparte, *American Ornithology; or, The Natural History of the Birds of the United States*, ed. Robert Jameson, 4 vols. (Edinburgh: Constable and Co., 1831). Note Samuels's emphasis on the domestic life of the birds.

"*Birdcraft* was hailed by . . . John Burroughs": John Burroughs to MOW, 8 July 1895 (MOW Autograph Album, FPL). See also Henry Van Dyke's letters of praise in the Autograph Album.

"Peterson's *Field Guide to the Birds*": Roger Tory Peterson, *Field Guide to the Birds* (New York: Houghton Mifflin, 1934). The only serious criticism of the book was leveled against its illustrations. C. Hart Merriam, reviewing the book in *Science* (n.s. 1 [1895]), wrote that "on opening Mrs. Wright's *Birdcraft*, fresh from the press, one is likely to exclaim 'what horrible pictures!' and wonder how a reputable publisher or author could permit such atrocious daubs to deface a well printed book. . . . The colored plates are execrable. Most of them are cheap, coarse, dauby caricatures, taken second-hand from Audubon, who would turn in his grave if he saw them" (635–36). In a 23 June 1895 letter to Allen, Wright responded to Merriam's review, noting that *Birdcraft* was "selling gayly" despite the poor quality of the plates. "I did all I could and succeeded in getting some of the most risky colours done in halftone. But I am glad to say that they really do help beginners, who see shape & general effect rather than detail, in spite of the fact that the wrens look as if they had taken a bath in ginger tea, & the female tanager was wrongly marked. Lots of people have written me to the effect that they have placed birds by the ('execrable plates' *Merriam*) pictures, that had puzzled them for years. Considering Dr. Merriam's natural disposition, I think his notice far better than I had hoped for. In fact if I had hoped at all in his direction it was that he would let me serenely alone" (Ornithology Dept., American Museum of Natural History [AMNH]). Macmillan hired Louis Agassiz Fuertes to prepare eighty new plates for the second edition of *Birdcraft*, which appeared in 1897. Unfortunately, these plates also failed to satisfy Wright, who described them as "simply *awful*" in a 26 October 1897 letter to George Brett. In a follow-up letter, dated 12 November 1897, Wright told Brett: "I am sorry to say that the advance criticism of my ornithological friends, coupled with my knowledge of what the new Birdcraft pictures *might* be, and what they are, has done much to destroy my interest in my work" (Macmillan Company Records, Box 18, NYPL).

9 "In October, after Allen published": MOW to J. A. Allen, 18 October 1894 (Ornithology Dept., AMNH). In his review, Allen called *Friendship* "charming" and noted that Wright's "frequent allusions to birds have a poetic setting and a background that render her book one of unusual literary merit and peculiarly fascinating to every lover of nature. . . . In general her allusions to the varied objects of nature, whether animals or plants, or things inanimate, are wonderfully truthful and show not only keen powers of observation but broad culture" (*The Auk* 11 [1894]: 314).

"The following March, she again thanked Allen": MOW to J. A. Allen, 11 March 1895 (Ornithology Dept., AMNH).

"In *Birdcraft*, for instance": MOW, *Birdcraft: A Field Book of Two Hundred Song, Game, and Water Birds*, 7th ed. (New York: Macmillan, 1909), xiii.

"And in *Flowers and Ferns in Their Haunts*": MOW, *Flowers and Ferns in Their Haunts* (New York: Macmillan, 1901), vii–ix.

10   "in *Mile Stones in Our Life-Journey*": Osgood, *Mile Stones*, 318.

"Liberty Hyde Bailey": Liberty Hyde Bailey, *The Nature-Study Idea* (New York: Doubleday, Page, and Co., 1903), 4. For more on Bailey, see Philip Dorf, *Liberty Hyde Bailey: An Informal Biography* (Ithaca, N.Y.: Cornell Univ. Press, 1956); and Andrew Denny Rodgers III, *Liberty Hyde Bailey: A Story of American Plant Sciences* (New York: Hafnet Publishing Co., 1965).

"For her 1897 bird class": "Tribute to Mabel Osgood Wright Is Read at Memorial Services," n.s., n.d., n.p. (CAS Records, BPL); "Sixtieth Anniversary of the Founding of the Audubon Society, State of Connecticut," Typescript (CAS Records, BPL). Wright detailed her teaching method in an essay for educators: "In teaching children I believe in striving to humanize the bird as far as is consistent with absolute truth, that the child may, through its own love of home, parents, and its various desires, be able to appreciate the corresponding traits in the bird.... Choose four or five [mounted] birds, not more for one day, take them outdoors, and place them in positions that shall resemble their natural haunts as much as possible.... Let the children look at them near by and then at a distance, so that a sense of proportion and color value will be developed unconsciously" (MOW, "A Bird Class for Children," *Bird-Lore* 1 [1899]: 100–101).

"according to Robert Henry Welker": Robert Henry Welker, *Birds and Men: American Birds in Science, Art, Literature, and Conservation, 1800–1900* (Cambridge, Mass.: Harvard Univ. Press, 1955), 189. Although Wright was christened Mabel, her name at home was "Tommy" for many years, according to one source. Similarly, Wright used her middle name ("Gray") in the title of her 1907 book, *Gray Lady and the Birds* ("Passing of Mabel Osgood Wright, Noted Novelist and Naturalist, Recalls Highlights of Her Splendid Life," *Bridgeport Sunday Post*, 22 July 1934, n.p. [CAS Records, BMS]).

"Two of her other children's books": Chapman also read and made corrections to *Tommy-Anne* in draft (MOW to Chapman, 17 June 1896 [Ornithology Dept., AMNH]). In *A World of Watchers* (New York: Knopf, 1986), his history of birdwatching, Joseph Kastner claims that

Wright "owed a good deal to her collaborators" (166) on *Citizen Bird*, but many of the 250 letters Wright and Coues exchanged during and after their collaboration reveal Wright's contribution to be the larger, a fact Coues wished to hide. On 11 March 1897, Coues wrote to Wright: "I made a very close study of it [the manuscript], during the three weeks I did nothing else, with no other idea than to carry your own plan and style to perfection. I could not have devised such a thing myself—but I will wager a lunch with you, next time I am in N.Y., that nobody can even pick out the three or four biographies I put in! . . . We are so inextricably interwoven through the book that nobody will ever be able to 'sort these babies out' " (MOW Autograph Album, FPL). On 6 August 1897, following the release of *Citizen Bird*, he then reminded Wright, "By the way, never give away the secret of the respective shares of authorship of C.B. There is already much guessing about it, always wide of the mark. I shall maintain impenetrability on that point, & you will be wise to do the same. Then the glamour of mystery will surround the book like a halo, in addition to its other fine points, and set tongues wagging & pens wriggling, & the publishers will rejoice accordingly" (MOW Autograph Album, FPL). In a letter to Julia Stockton (Mrs. Edward Robins), Coues was less charitable about Wright's role in the collaboration, noting that "I could have swatted those children [portrayed in the book] into the middle of next week, during the whole time I was working on the MS., but I knew the public Mrs. Wright was addressing, and consequently encouraged the young ones in their behavior. The result is the most popular and best selling bird book for children ever written" (Paul Russell Cutright and Michael J. Brodhead, *Elliott Coues: Naturalist and Frontier Historian* [Urbana: Univ. of Illinois Press, 1981], 387). Wright described Coues as "an odd stick" in an 8 August 1897 letter to George Brett (Macmillan Company Records, Box 18, NYPL).

"her vocal criticism of such 'nature fakers' ": According to Frank Chapman in *Autobiography of a Bird-Lover* (New York: D. Appleton-Century Co., 1933), "as a resident of Stamford, [Long] made the welcoming address at the annual meeting of the Connecticut Audubon Society, held in that city May 25, 1901. . . . At the conclusion of the meeting he was introduced to Mabel Osgood Wright, President of the Society. 'Wright, Wright,' he said, 'you're the bird woman, aren't you? It seems to me that I have a letter from you at home, but I haven't read it yet.' 'Well, it couldn't be from me,' Mrs. Wright replied with icy clearness, 'for I never heard of you before' " (183). See also MOW, "Nature as a Field for Fiction," *New York Times Book Review*, 9 December 1905, 872. For more on the "nature fakers," see Ralph Lutts, *The Nature Fakers: Wildlife, Science, and Sentiment* (Golden, Colo.: Fulcrum, 1990); and Lisa

Mighetto, *Wild Animals and American Environmental Ethics* (Tucson: Univ. of Arizona Press, 1991).

"As she noted in *Tommy-Anne and the Three Hearts*": MOW, *Tommy-Anne and the Three Hearts* (New York: Macmillan, 1896): half-title. In a 16 May 1899 letter, Wright told George Brett that it was "a difficult thing to weave a wide range of science and natural history in a story book and keep all the facts in order" (Macmillan Company Records, Box 18, NYPL). Later, on 21 October, Henry Van Dyke wrote to Wright that *Wabeno, the Magician* "is fascinating even to an old boy like me. There is so much in it that I didn't even *think* I knew. It is all so clearly and simply told, with so much imagination, and best of all, it's true.—Your feeling that the children of today can appreciate the idea of a flowering creation from vital seeds, and that it will mean far more to them than the old notion of manufacture by fiat, is certainly right. I know my children will enjoy this book, but they can't have it till I am through with it" (MOW Autograph Album, FPL).

11 "*Elizabeth and Her German Garden*": Elizabeth von Arnim (Mary Annette Beauchamp Russell), *Elizabeth and Her German Garden*, intro. by Elizabeth Jane Howard (1898; London: Virago, 1985). See also the sequel, *The Solitary Summer* (New York: Macmillan, 1899); *The Enchanted April*, intro. by Terence de Vere White (1922; London: Virago, 1986), recently adapted for the screen; and Karen Usborne, *"Elizabeth": The Author of "Elizabeth and Her German Garden"* (London: Bodley Head, 1986).

"Wright later recalled": "Mabel Osgood Wright Recalls Pleasures." Wright refers to *Elizabeth and Her German Garden* on pages 87 and 88 of *The Garden of a Commuter's Wife*.

"semiautobiographical 'Barbara' books": Beverly Seaton discusses *The Garden of a Commuter's Wife* and *The Garden, You, and I* (1906) in "The Garden Autobiography," *Garden History* 7.1 (spring 1979): 101–20. See also Virginia Lopez Begg, "Mabel Osgood Wright: The Friendship of Nature and the Commuter's Wife," *Journal of the New England Garden History Society* 5 (fall 1997): 35–41.

"When 'Barbara's' identity was finally revealed": "Mabel Osgood Wright Recalls Pleasures"; "Concerning Anonymities," *Bookman* 23 (March 1906): 7; "The Lounger," *Critic* 48 (1906): 296–98.

"As the *New York Times* commented": *New York Times Book Review*, 7 August 1909, 477.

"many of Wright's fictional works offer valuable glimpses": Especially interesting from a biographical perspective is *The Woman Errant* (New

York: Macmillan, 1904), in which a female physician contributes to the death of her son by choosing not to administer the proper vaccine for diphtheria. Wright attributes the misdiagnosis to the character's "professional pride and mother love wrestling together," but the incident also suggests that Wright may have been attempting to justify her own decision to abandon a career in medicine for a more traditional one as wife and homemaker, her writing and conservation work notwithstanding (318–23). Wright's last novel, *Eudora's Men* (New York: Macmillan, 1931), raises similar issues.

12 "As Paul Brooks has noted": Paul Brooks, *Speaking for Nature: How Literary Naturalists from Henry Thoreau to Rachel Carson Have Shaped America* (Boston: Houghton Mifflin, 1980), 168.

"After the first Audubon Society": See Frank Graham Jr., *The Audubon Ark: A History of the National Audubon Society* (New York: Knopf, 1990); Robin W. Doughty, *Feather Fashions and Bird Preservation: A Study in Nature Protection* (Berkeley: Univ. of California Press, 1975); Felton Gibbons and Deborah Strom, *Neighbors to the Birds: A History of Birdwatching in America* (New York: Norton, 1988); Oliver H. Orr Jr., *Saving American Birds: T. Gilbert Pearson and the Founding of the Audubon Movement* (Gainesville: Univ. Press of Florida, 1992); and Mark V. Barrow, *A Passion for Birds: American Ornithology after Audubon* (Princeton: Princeton Univ. Press, 1998).

"As Wright explained in a 1923 article": MOW, "Conn. Audubon Society Holds Annual Meet," *Fairfield News*, 9 June 1923, 5. An active member of the D.A.R., Wright first read her poem "A Hymn to Our Flag" at a regional meeting of the group in 1898. On 4 July 1916 the "Connecticut Hymn of the Flag" was sung for the first time to the Wright's own music, and in February 1917 the Connecticut legislature reviewed a bill designating it the state anthem (D.A.R., Eunice Dennie Burr Chapter Records, FHS); "Outstanding Figures among Women of State in Last Half Century Named," *Bridgeport Post* [4 July 1926]: n.p. [MOW Vertical File, FHS]).

"the Audubon Society of Connecticut": The society's official name at this time was "Audubon Society, State of Connecticut." Due to an oversight, the society was not formally incorporated until 13 June 1914. See "Sixtieth Anniversary."

"Wright . . . was elected president": Wright was also instrumental in the founding of the Fairfield Garden Club in 1915 and an informal Reading Club in the 1920s. See Mrs. Robert Leach and Mrs. John Field, *History of the Fairfield Garden Club, 1915–1948* (Fairfield, Conn.: Fairfield Garden Club, 1948).

"The first annual report": Audubon Society of Connecticut, *Annual Report*, June 1898 (CAS Records, BMS).

"to establish 'Bird-Day' ": The first Bird Day was held in the Oil City, Pennsylvania, public school system in 1894 at the suggestion of superintendent Charles A. Babcock; Connecticut created Bird Day in 1899. Bird Day was modeled after Arbor Day, begun in 1872 by Julius Sterling Morton. See Charles A. Babcock, *Bird Day: How to Prepare for It* (New York: Silver, Burdett and Co., 1901); "Bird Day for Children," *New York Times*, 21 April 1901, 20; and T. S. Palmer, *Bird Day in Schools* (U.S. Dept. of Agriculture, Div. of Biological Survey, Circular 17 [Washington, D.C.: Government Printing Office, 1896]). See also *The Auk* 11 (1894): 342; *The Auk* 13 (1896): 349; and *Forest and Stream* 47 (18 July 1896): 41.

"During its first years of existence": Information on the membership and activities of the society can be found in the occasional reports published in the Audubon department of *Bird-Lore* during the magazine's early years.

13 "Defending the secretaries": MOW, "WORK! And after That More Work," *Bird-Lore* 4 (1902): 103-4.

"Wright told Frank Chapman": MOW to Frank Chapman, 11 July 1905 (Ornithology Dept., AMNH).

"she wrote to Audubon leader T. Gilbert Pearson": MOW to T. Gilbert Pearson, 5 September 1913 (NAS Records, Box A-64, NYPL).

"National Association of Audubon Societies": Not until 1940 did the association change its name to the National Audubon Society. The relationship between the state societies and the national association has been a source of tension since the formation of the national committee in 1901. At that time, committee members agreed that the strong state societies would preserve their autonomy, while the national committee would merely serve as an umbrella organization, linking independent state societies that shared common aims. Over time, however, this arrangement produced confusion among the general public, as a 21 February 1920 letter from MOW to T. Gilbert Pearson demonstrates. "A great many people do not distinguish between the National Assoc. and the *Audubon Soc. State of Conn.*," according to Wright.

They say to me "we are members of *The* Audubon Society."
"Which one?" I ask.
"Why the one in this state of course. But you never ask us to your meetings."
I follow the matter up and find they belong to the N. Assoc.
(NAS Records, Box A-91, NYPL)

The national association has gradually grown in power, financial strength, and membership since 1901, and today only eleven state Audubon societies exist independently of the National Audubon Society, which has approximately five hundred and seventy thousand members in forty states. Interestingly, as early as 1903 MOW recognized that the future of bird protection would require more than just *national* associations. "Not only national but international cooperation is the only cement that will hold together the stones of individual effort that are to build the protective wall against which the shot of plume- and pot-hunter is to rattle in vain," she wrote in "The Spread of Bird Protection" (*Bird-Lore* 5 [1903]: 37).

"When she finally resigned": T. Gilbert Pearson to MOW, 2 November 1928 (NAS Records, Box A-136, NYPL).

14   "according to Oliver H. Orr Jr.": Orr, *Saving American Birds*, 128.

"magazine founded by Frank Chapman": Wright's correspondence with Chapman reveals the central role she played as an administrator in the first years of the Audubon movement. "I used to have sometimes 20 letters a week," she wrote Chapman on 20 August 1903, "but since Mr. Dutcher has been letter answerer for the National Committee they have almost ceased; in fact I have had but two in a month. Also I think that people are getting to realize that the societies are state affairs and are now more apt to write to the nearest secretary than to me" (Ornithology Dept., AMNH).

"In his *Autobiography*": Chapman, *Autobiography of a Bird-Lover*, 188. Contributors to *Bird-Lore* during the journal's early years included John Burroughs, Henry Van Dyke, Bradford Torrey, Ernest Thompson Seton, Olive Thorne Miller, Florence Merriam Bailey, and William Brewster. In 1935 *Bird-Lore* was bought by the National Association of Audubon Societies; in 1941 its name was changed to *Audubon Magazine*; and in 1961 its name was shortened simply to *Audubon*. For more on *Bird-Lore*, see Roger Tory Peterson, "The Evolution of a Magazine," *Audubon*, January 1973, 46-51.

"Wright informed the readers": MOW, "The Responsibility of the Audubon Society," *Bird-Lore* 1 (1899): 136-37.

"She repeated this claim": MOW, "Fees and Pledges," *Bird-Lore* 2 (1900): 64.

15   " 'The Conducting of Audubon Societies' ": MOW, "The Conducting of Audubon Societies," *Bird-Lore* 1 (1899): 64.

" 'The Law and the Bird' ": MOW, "The Law and the Bird," *Bird-Lore* 1 (1899): 204.

"Putting the matter more plainly": MOW, "Wanted—The Truth," *Bird-Lore* 2 (1900): 33.

"she wrote in 1903": MOW, "The Literature of Bird Protection," *Bird-Lore* 5 (1903): 138.

"a wide range of legislative initiatives": See MOW to William Dutcher, 28 December 1900 (NAS Records, Box A-6, NYPL); B. S. Bowdish, "The Relation of the Audubon Movement to the Sportsman," *Scientific American* 98.9 (29 February 1908): 139; Willard G. VanName to MOW, 13 January 1908 (CAS Records, BMS); Rep. George L. Lilley to Helen Glover, 6 February 1908 (CAS Records, BMS); MOW, *Annual Report to the National Association of Audubon Societies*, Draft [1911] (NAS Records, Box A-43, NYPL); MOW to T. Gilbert Pearson, 8 May 1912 and 8 October 1912 (NAS Records, Box A-50, NYPL); MOW, draft letter regarding preservation of the bald eagle, n.d. (CAS Records, BMS). MOW to T. Gilbert Pearson, 30 May 1919 (NAS Records, Box A-87, NYPL). Wright was following in a long tradition of concern for game laws in Connecticut, which passed the first game law in America in 1677. See T. S. Palmer, *Chronology and Index of the More Important Events in American Game Protection, 1776-1911*, U.S. Dept. of Agriculture, Bureau of Biological Survey, Bulletin 41 (Washington, D.C.: Government Printing Office, 1912).

16   "her efforts at the local level": Another example of her success in such endeavors was the interest she took in Fairfield's Oak Lawn Cemetery, whose directors she first approached in 1907, convinced that the grounds had become too cluttered and overgrown. According to Thomas J. Farnham, Wright and her sister Agnes hoped to make the cemetery less rustic and more like a park; they wanted to see it become "more open, more spacious, more pastoral, more attuned to the modern tastes" (*The Oak Lawn Cemetery* [Fairfield, Conn.: Oak Lawn Cemetery Assoc., 1993], 13). By 1914 Wright had begun advocating for cemeteries to be used as bird sanctuaries, an idea also taken up by the national association, from whom Wright felt she did not receive proper credit (MOW to T. Gilbert Pearson, 1 January 1916 [NAS Records, Box A-78, NYPL]). For more on the scenic cemetery movement, see Neil Harris, *The Artist in American Society: The Formative Years, 1790-1860* (1966; Chicago: Univ. of Chicago Press, 1982), 200-208; Hans Huth, *Nature and the American: Three Centuries of Changing Attitudes* (1957; Lincoln: Univ. of Nebraska Press, 1990), 66-70; and David Schuyler, "The Evolution of the Anglo-American Rural Cemetery," *Journal of Garden History* 4.3 (July–September 1984): 291-304, part of a special issue on "Cemetery and Garden."

"arguing in the pages of *Bird-Lore*": MOW, "Song Bird Reservations," *Bird-Lore* 3 (1901): 114.

"By 1910 she had grown even more insistent": MOW, "Bird-Cities-of-Refuge," *Bird-Lore* 12 (1910): 159–60.

"The masque, written by Percy Mackaye": Percy Mackaye, *Sanctuary: A Bird Masque* (New York: Frederick A. Stokes, 1914). The performance at the Astor Place Theater drew an audience of 2,000, a capacity crowd. See also Robert P. Allen's "The Wild-Life Sanctuary Movement in the United States" (*Bird-Lore* 36 [1934]), in which MOW says that she heard her father describe Mosswood as "The Sanctuary of the Birds" as early as 1862 (83). Allen incorrectly gives the date of the Meriden sanctuary's founding as 1911.

"In the minutes of the society": Connecticut Audubon Society, *Minutes*, 10 July 1914 (CAS Records, BPL).

"the recollections of an Audubon Society member": Deborah N. Glover, *Some of My Memories about the Audubon Society, State of Connecticut*, Typescript, July 1972 (CAS Records, BMS).

17 "Wright's ideal landscape": MOW, "Inviting the Birds and Wild Flowers," *Garden Magazine and Home Builder* 40 (1924): 108.

"Wright directed the planting": Wright's legacy in this area can be seen in part by such books as Stephen W. Kress, *The Audubon Society Guide to Attracting Birds* (New York: Scribner, 1985).

"Frank Chapman, writing in *Bird-Lore*": Frank Chapman, "Editorial," *Bird-Lore* 17 (1915): 297. In his article on "Collections of Birds in the United States and Canada" in *Fifty Years' Progress of American Ornithology, 1883–1933* (Lancaster, Pa.: American Ornithologists' Union, 1933), Chapman said that the Birdcraft Museum and Sanctuary "should be seen by every one contemplating the development of similar projects" (148).

"Helen Glover . . . in her annual report": Helen W. Glover, "Report of the Secretary of the Audubon Soc. State of Connecticut," Typescript, 1917–18 (CAS Records, BMS).

"when Edith Roosevelt was seeking": "MOW Recalls Pleasures." See also MOW to Helen Glover, 16 September 1923 (CAS Records, BPL). The Roosevelt Sanctuary, located adjacent to the president's grave, was established on land donated to the National Audubon Society by the Roosevelt family after Roosevelt's death in 1919. Wright, whom T. Gilbert Pearson asked to serve on the committee to select a fountain design for the sanctuary, thought the fountain "should represent the rigorous modern Rooseveltian side of conservation, not the sentimental & idealistic side." The sentimental sculpture of a lightly clothed nymphet and prepubescent boy that was selected, Wright protested, was "totally unfit for its purpose of being a Roosevelt memorial." See the exchange of letters between MOW and T. Gilbert Pearson (NAS Records, Boxes A-112 and A-113, NYPL).

18 "the removal of so-called 'problem species'": see John Burroughs, "Bird Enemies," *Century* 31 (1885): 270–74. Modern ecologists call this the "Mother Goose Syndrome," in which animals are designated "good" or "bad" depending on their perceived effects.

"In a 1922 letter to Wright": Frederic C. Walcott to MOW, 11 May 1922 (CAS Records, BMS).

"In the first three years": MOW, "Three Years After: Some Notes on Birdcraft Sanctuary, Fairfield, Conn.," *Bird-Lore* 20 (1918): 201–10.

"Wright claimed in an 1899 column": MOW, "The Law and the Bird," 203.

"in a later column": MOW, "Meditations on the Posting of Bird Laws," *Bird-Lore* 5 (1903): 205. See also MOW, "Encouraging Signs," *Bird-Lore* 3 (1901): 146.

"As Thomas R. Dunlap acknowledges": Thomas R. Dunlap, *Saving America's Wildlife* (Princeton: Princeton Univ. Press, 1988), 8.

19 "Landscape historian John Stilgoe": Stilgoe, *Borderland*, 296. For more on nativism and conservation, see Stephen R. Fox, *John Muir and His Legacy: The American Conservation Movement* (Boston: Little, Brown, 1981). Michael Pollan questions the philosophy behind the modern native-plant garden in "Against Nativism," *New York Times Magazine*, 15 May 1994, 52–55.

"Wright outlined the first part": MOW, "The Making of Birdcraft Sanctuary," *Bird-Lore* 17 (1915): 263.

" 'At Birdcraft,' she added later": MOW, "Little Stories from Birdcraft Sanctuary: I. A Hummingbird Waif," *Bird-Lore* 24 (1922): 195.

"the songbirds were driven away": Visitations numbered sixty-two hundred in its third year of operation (MOW, "Three Years After," 203).

"a collection Wright found to be": MOW, "Birdcraft Sanctuary: After Sixteen Years—Facts and Phantasy," *Bird-Lore* 32 (1930): 403.

"As one commentator noted": "God's Ten Acres for the Feathered Friends of Men in Fairfield Bird Sanctuary," *Bridgeport Telegram*, n.d., n.p. (CAS Records, BPL).

"Wright herself had proposed keeping": MOW, "The End of the Beginning—Wild Flowers and Hawks," *Bird-Lore* 26 (1924): 105–6.

20 "noted the . . . secretary": Connecticut Audubon Society, *Minutes*, 27 June 1957 (CAS Records, BPL).

"Eventually the society received": Connecticut Audubon Society, *Minutes*, 24 July 1958 (CAS Records, BPL). In 1958, a much smaller parcel of land was condemned by the Town of Fairfield for the Roger Ludlow High School (now Tomlinson Middle School), for which the society received $7,900 (*Minutes*, 15 December 1958).

"the constant hum of the thruway": The thruway greatly affected the number of migrating birds counted at the sanctuary, according to Bird-craft's warden, Frank Novak, speaking in 1970. "We do get some, but not what we used to get. We get approximately 100 different species now, whereas originally we used to get 250. . . . The thruway has driven them away to a great extent" (Frank Novak, Interview, Audiocassette, October 1970. [CAS Records, BPL]). The main offices of the Connecticut Audubon Society are now located at 2325 Burr Street in Fairfield.

"the loss of her husband in 1920": Obituary of James O. Wright, *New York Times*, 28 May 1920, 13.

"In a letter to T. Gilbert Pearson": MOW to T. Gilbert Pearson, 1 October 1920 (NAS Records, Box A-97, NYPL). For additional reactions to her husband's death, see MOW to Helen Glover, 1 July 1922 (CAS Records, BPL); MOW to Helen Glover, 19 August 1924 (CAS Records, BPL); and MOW to Frank Chapman, 3 December 1932 (Ornithology Dept., AMNH).

"By 1916 the couple sold Mosswood": "Mabel Osgood Wright Recalls Pleasures." After being used as schoolhouse and then falling into disuse, Mosswood was eventually destroyed and replaced with 136 luxury apartments known as Mosswood Condominiums.

21 "her 1925 essay, 'A Tired Woman's Roses' ": MOW, "A Tired Woman's Roses," *The 1925 American Rose Annual*, ed. J. Horace McFarland (Harrisburg, Pa.: American Rose Society, 1925), 25.

"Initially Wright had planned to publish": See Marble. The first American edition of *Charlotte Temple* was printed in Philadelphia by D. Humphries in 1794. In letters to T. Gilbert Pearson, Wright describes *My New York* as "the greatest hit of my whole life!" (16 December 1926) and says "it has brought me more general recognition than everything else that I have done, which is pretty good for one of my age" (25 October 1926 [misdated 1936]). Both letters appear in NAS Records, Box A-127, NYPL. Wright received a stream of appreciative letters about *My New York* from 1926 through 1928, which fill her Autograph Album (FPL).

"As a final tribute to Wright": "State Honors Woman Writer," *Bridge-port Post*, 23 June 1926, n.p. (MOW Vertical File, FHS).

"She died at age seventy-five": Death certificate, Connecticut Department of Health; Obituary of MOW, *New York Times*, 18 July 1934, 17.

"One of Wright's comments": MOW, *Friendship*, 112. Subsequent citations to this edition of *Friendship* will appear parenthetically in the text.

"Thomas J. Lyon has argued": Thomas J. Lyon, *This Incomperable Lande: A Book of American Nature Writing* (Boston: Houghton Mifflin, 1989), 3.

"Wright follows this same seasonal progression in other texts": See, for instance, "Birds and Seasons in My Garden," a series of articles that appeared throughout the year in *Bird-Lore* 13 (1911). A similar series appeared in *Bird-Lore* 9 (1907).

22 "As *Popular Science Monthly* noted": *Popular Science Monthly* 46 (February 1895): 562.

23 "Wright makes this point explicitly": MOW, "The Truce of the Year: Winter, Dogs, and Books," *Critic* 44 (February 1904): 138.

"As John Holman ... once noted": "Eloquent Words for Mrs. Wright," *Bridgeport Post*, 25 January 1935, n.p. (MOW Vertical File, FHS).

24 "a 1905 lecture about colonial history": MOW, *The Value of Colonial Influence* (New York: [National Society of the Colonial Dames of America,] 1905), 26. In *The Garden of a Commuter's Wife*, Wright notes that in her youth she read Longfellow's *Song of Hiawatha* (1855) and after reading Schoolcraft fancied herself descended from American Indians (180-81).

25 "Annette Kolodny, Vera Norwood": Annette Kolodny, *The Land before Her: Fantasy and Experience of the American Frontiers, 1630-1860* (Chapel Hill: Univ. of North Carolina Press, 1984); Vera Norwood, *Made from This Earth: American Women and Nature* (Chapel Hill: Univ. of North Carolina Press, 1993).

26 "Leo Marx in *Machine in the Garden*": Leo Marx, *The Machine in the Garden: Technology and the Pastoral Ideal in America* (New York: Oxford Univ. Press, 1964).

"In *Gray Lady and the Birds*": MOW, *Gray Lady and the Birds: Stories of the Bird Year for Home and School* (New York: Macmillan, 1907), xi.

27 " 'The Making of Birdcraft Sanctuary' ": MOW, "Making of Bird-craft," 273.

A NEW ENGLAND MAY-DAY

29 "That it was May": Geoffrey Chaucer (c. 1343–1400), *The Romaunt of the Rose* (n.d.), l. 51.

31 "This year April has overslept": 1893. [Wright's note]

"the fringed gentian, set by Bryant": William Cullen Bryant (1794–1878), "To the Fringed Gentian" (1832).

"yet it is May-day": According to Polydore Vergil (1470?–1555?), Roman youths used to spend the Calends, or first day, of May dancing and singing in honor of Flora, the goddess of fruits and flowers.

"the guinea-stamp of Nature": A former British gold coin worth one pound and five pence.

32 "the jaunty Robert of Lincoln": Named after Robert Bloet (d. 1123), bishop of Lincoln. Cf. William Cullen Bryant's poem "Robert of Lincoln" (1855). In the 1909 edition of *Birdcraft*, Wright says, "Bryant's poem on Robert of Lincoln contains a good description of the bird's plumage, but it is too precise and measured to express the rapture of the song. It may describe a stuffed Bobolink, but never a wild, living one" (166). In an interview, Wright recalled that when William Cullen Bryant visited Mosswood during her girlhood, she told him that she knew "Robert of Lincoln" by heart. "He smiled as if pleased and began to repeat the poem, slowly and without inflection of any kind," Wright recalled. " 'Why doesn't he speak quicker and make the bob'o'link fly faster?' was the thought that has always remained." See Marble.

33 "Its notes have been translated": By John Burroughs (1837–1921) in *Wake-Robin* (1871), his first book of nature essays.

34 "the course of the river": Mill River.

35 "the Moon of Leaves": Originally, a new month started on the day of the new moon.

"The word of the sun to the sky": Algernon Charles Swinburne (1837–1909), "Triads" (1878), I.1–4.

WHEN ORCHARDS BLOOM

37 "The robin and the bluebird piping loud": Henry Wadsworth Longfellow (1807–82), "The Birds of Killingworth" (1863), ll. 9–12.

39 "Ceres, who has been a laggard for weeks": The Roman goddess of agriculture.

"Pomona, anxious for her harvest": The Roman goddess of fruit.

"rosy as Aurora's fingertips": The Roman goddess of the dawn.

THE ROMAUNT OF THE ROSE

45 "I saw the sweetest flower": John Keats (1795-1821), "To a Friend Who Sent Me Some Roses" (1817), ll. 5-7.

48 "the feuds of Lancaster and York": Otherwise known as the Wars of the Roses (1455-85), the Civil Wars in England between the House of Lancaster (whose badge was the Red Rose) and the House of York (whose badge was the White Rose). The Wars ended in the triumph of Henry Tudor (1457-1509), head of the House of Lancaster, at Bosworth.

49 "Mephisto's name and cloak": Mephistopheles, the devil in the Faust legend to whom Faust sold his soul.

"roses for Gargantua": A giant king famous for his appetite, the hero of the satire *Gargantua and Pantagruel* (1535) by François Rabelais (c. 1494–c. 1553).

"Ask General Jacqueminot": This rose and others with formal names can be identified in a number of guides to roses, including Peter Beales, *Classic Roses* (New York: Holt, Rinehart, and Winston, 1985), and Brent C. Dickerson, *The Old Rose Advisor* (Portland, Oreg.: Timber Press, 1992).

50 "A walk bordered with box": An evergreen tree or shrub of the genus *Buxus*, esp. *B. sempervirens*.

"snowballs ... almost hid a fallen apple tree": Any of several plants or shrubs having rounded clusters of white flowers, esp. a cultivated variety of *Viburnum opulus*.

51 "Lothair received from Corisande": Characters in the novel *Lothair* (1870) by Benjamin Disraeli (1804-81).

THE GARDENS OF THE SEA

53 "On the wide marsh": James Russell Lowell (1819-91), "Summer Storm" (1839), ll. 13-14.

55 "stiff ebon ooze": Ebony; black.

56 "rough-fronded brakes": Any of several ferns, esp. bracken, *Pteridium aquilinum*.

"trig as an hussar": Trim or neat as a horseman of the Hungarian light cavalry, organized during the fifteenth century.

57 "cat-tail flag": Any of various plants having long, bladelike leaves, such as an iris (genus *Iris*) or cattail (genus *Typha*).

58 "Next came the vernal equinox": The beginning of spring, about 21 March. The vernal equinox is the moment at which the sun passes through the point at which the ecliptic intersects the celestial equator, the sun having a northerly motion.

"She brings us fish": Alexander Wilson (1766–1813), "The Fish Hawk, or Osprey" (1814), ll. 25–26.

A SONG OF SUMMER

61 "Shine! shine! shine!": Walt Whitman (1819–92), "Out of the Cradle Endlessly Rocking" (1860), ll. 32–34.

63 "the Julian calendar": The Julian Calendar, introduced by Julius Caesar in 46 B.C., was used in Europe until the introduction of the Gregorian Calendar by Pope Gregory XIII in 1582.

"the summer solstice": 21 or 22 June, when the sun reaches its extreme northern point in the ecliptic and appears to stand still (Lat. *sol*, sun; *sistit*, stands) before it turns back on its apparent course; midsummer.

"the festival of St. John the Baptist": 24 June.

"We two stand together": Though Wright often uses the first-person plural to include her reader in her walks, here she also seems to be referring to a specific companion, probably her husband James, who likely also plays the role of "Adam" later in this essay.

64 "last year's dock": Any of various weedy plants of the genus *Rumex*, having clusters of small greenish or reddish flowers.

"Pan . . . blowing softly through his oaten pipe": Pan is the Greek god of pastures, forests, flocks, and herds. He is represented with the upper part of a man and the body and legs of a goat. Pan-pipes, an ancient wind instrument, are said to have derived from the reed into which the nymph Syrinx was transformed when fleeing from Pan's amorous intentions.

65 "a bunch of simples": Medicinal plants.

"Lydia Languish": Character in *The Rivals* (1775), a play by Richard Brinsley Sheridan (1751–1816).

65 "when the malarial breath steams from the soil": Malaria, a disease transmitted by the bite of an infected mosquito, was long believed to have been transmitted through bad air (Ital. *mala aria*, bad air).

66 "O truth painter of Barbizon": The Barbizon School was a group of French landscape painters active between 1830 and 1880 in and around Barbizon, a village about thirty miles south of Paris. They include Theodore Rousseau (1812–67), Charles Francois Daubigny (1817–78), Narcisse Virgile Diaz de la Pena (1808–76), and Constant Troyon (1810–65). Unlike the classical landscapes of Nicolas Poussin (1594–1665) and the picturesque scenes of such romantic painters as Eugene Delacroix (1798–1863), the paintings of the Barbizon School were an attempt to capture the truth of the local landscape by using muted colors and reproducing the effects of twilight.

"the New World's Angelus": The bell rung as a call to recite the Angelus, a Roman Catholic devotional prayer recited thrice daily, usually at 6 A.M., noon, and 6 P.M. The prayer honors the Annunciation and begins with the Latin words *Angelus Domini nunttiavit Mariae*.

67 "Arachne is napping": In Greek mythology, a maiden who was transformed into a spider by Athena for challenging her to a weaving contest. Hence *Arachnida*, the class of arthropods that includes spiders.

68 "Woof of the fen, ethereal gauze": Henry David Thoreau, *A Week on the Concord and Merrimack Rivers* (1849). The first line of the poem is incorrect as cited here; the correct line reads "Woof of the *sun*, ethereal gauze" (emphasis added).

69 "Adam, replacing the Biblical heel with a stone, promptly bruises the serpent's head": Clearly, not all of nature is on friendly terms with Wright.

"Sing willow, willow, willow": Part of the refrain of Thomas Procter's "A Louer Approuing His Lady Vnkinde" (1578). The phrase also appears in "When Fancie First Fram'd Our Likings in Leve," by Thomas Deloney (1560?–1600).

70 "Rest is the even-song of summer": Unidentified.

FEATHERED PHILOSOPHERS

71 "You cannot with a scalpel find": Unidentified.

73 "as its eulogist Michelet says": Jules Michelet (1798–1874), *The Bird* (1869), 87.

74 "chronicler of the Val Sainte Veronique": Unidentified.

"We are what suns and winds and waters make us": The first four lines of "Regeneration," by Walter Savage Landor (1775–1864).

" 'Knock at this window,' said Death": Unidentified.

75   "when Sterne tore vainly at the wires": Laurence Sterne (1713–68), *A Sentimental Journey through France and Italy* (1768).

"The siskin was of a Byronic mood": Rebellious; after George Gordon, Lord Byron (1788–1824).

77   "Bradford Torrey has noted this trait": Bradford Torrey (1843–1912), American nature writer.

"wearing Lord Baltimore's colours": Wright tells the following story in the 1909 edition of *Birdcraft*: "George Calvert, the first Baron Baltimore, who penned the charter of settlement in 1632 of the country which now comprises the states of Delaware and Maryland (a grant which fructified later for the benefit of his son), is the subject of the tradition which still lingers in Maryland, and has sufficient facts for a foundation to be credible. The story says that Calvert, worn out and discouraged by the various trials and rigours of temperature in his Newfoundland colony, in 1628 visited the Virginia settlement. He explored the waters of the Chesapeake, with its noble tributaries and delicious climate, and found the shores and woods teeming with birds, and among them great flocks of Orioles, who so cheered him by their song and colour [black and orange] that he took them as good omens and adopted the colours for his own" (172–73). Calvert (1580–1632) died before the charter of settlement became official. His eldest son, Cecil Calvert, 2nd Baron Baltimore, (c. 1605–75), carried out his plans.

78   "Wise Mother Nature": Nine years later, in 1903, Wright would comment: "Why is Nature always spoken of as feminine—Mother Nature—which indicates the incomplete, the partial? Nature is one and indivisible, the eternal male and female." See her "Life Outdoors and Its Effect upon Literature," *Critic* 42 (April 1903): 308–11.

79   "On the top of the trellis . . . was a young cowbird": Wright elaborates on the cowbird in the 1909 edition of *Birdcraft*: "When the laying impulse seizes them, they slyly deposit the egg in the nest of some smaller bird. This shows forethought, however; for there is less likelihood of the eggs being thrust out, and it also obtains a greater share of warmth than the other eggs in the nest and hatches more rapidly" (168).

NATURE'S CALM

83   "The mountain brows, the rocks": Alcman, ancient Greek poet. Sir Edwin Arnold (1832–1904), British poet and translator.

86 "the northern Aurora": Aurora borealis, bands of light sometimes visible in the night skies of the northern regions. They are thought to be caused by the ejection of charged particles into the magnetic field of the earth. Wright's usage here differs from her later mention of Aurora, when she refers not to the night sky but to the early morning. In Greek mythology, Eos (Lat. *Aurora*) is the goddess of the dawn.

87 "In their yearly revelry": Aristophanes (c. 448–380 B.C.), *The Frogs*. The translation is the metrical version published by John Hookham Frere (1769–1846) in 1839.

89 "Or, weird and wee, sits Puck himself": Unidentified.

"treasure-laden tomb of Nineveh": Ancient capital of the Assyrian empire, on the Tigris River opposite the site of modern Mosul, Iraq.

90 "Was it Palissy?": Bernard Palissy (1510–89), French potter and enameller, whose "Palissy Ware" features models of fish, reptiles, shells, flowers, leaves, and other natural forms colored and enamelled in high relief.

"the Virgin's lilies": In Christian art, the lily is a symbol of chastity, innocence, and purity. Pictures of the Annunciation sometimes feature the Virgin kneeling in prayer before a vase containing a lily.

"soft folds of tulle": A fine, netted fabric of silk, often used for veils.

"Doré . . . the Wandering Jew": Gustave Doré (1832–83), *The Legend of the Wandering Jew: A Series of Twelve Designs* (1880).

THE STORY OF A GARDEN

91 "Nature, as far as in her lies": Alfred, Lord Tennyson (1809–92), "On a Mourner" (1832), ll. 1–2.

93 "as Bacon says": Francis Bacon (1561–1626), "Of Gardens" (1625).

"This man, even when a little boy": Her father, Samuel Osgood.

96 "If you would keep the wild birds in your garden": Wright often repeated this advice in her writings, particularly after the opening of Birdcraft Sanctuary in 1914.

"the men of Killingworth": Farmers who, in Longfellow's poem, slaughter all the birds of the town for feeding on their crops.

97 "as the Mussulman does his minaret": Moslem (Turk. *musulman*, probably an alteration of Ar. *muslim*).

98 "the fatal Heimweh": Homesickness (Ger.).

100 "First a little slender line": Unidentified.

101 "to quizz you": British usage: to poke fun at, mock.

"there lies the garden's eye": Cf. Henry David Thoreau (1817–1862) in "The Ponds" chapter of *Walden* (1854): "A lake is the landscape's most beautiful and expressive feature. It is earth's eye; looking into which the beholder measures the depth of his own nature."

"*le soulier de Notre Dame*": Lady's-slipper.

102 "All *hate* abandon ye who enter here!": Variation on the words encountered by Dante Alighieri (1265–1321) over the gateway to hell in Canto III of the *Inferno*: "Abandon every hope, ye that enter." Beatrice (d. 1290), Dante's love, is celebrated and idealized in the *Vita Nuova* and *Divina Commedia*.

RUSTLING WINGS

103 "All the feathered airy nation": Aristophanes' *The Birds*, translated and versified by Frere in 1840.

107 "angle and sweep over the Sound": the Long Island Sound.

110 "flies with a quick, sharp movement": Unidentified.

111 "The Greeks had their Spring Swallow Song": See Athenaeus, *Deipnosophistae* (*The Sophists at Dinner*), VIII.360.

112 "Turn, turn my wheel!": Unidentified.

THE LOOM OF AUTUMN

113 "There she weaves both night and day": Alfred, Lord Tennyson, "The Lady of Shalott" (1842), ll. 37–38.

116 "Midas must have left the underworld some day": The legendary king of Phrygia who asked the gods that everything he touched might be turned to gold.

117 "a moral sketch by Hogarth": William Hogarth (1697–1764), British painter and engraver, whose series of prints, such as *A Harlot's Progress* (1732), *A Rake's Progress* (1735), and *Marriage a la Mode* (1745), employ details as narrative devices.

118 "the white grass of Parnassus": A mountain in Greece sacred to Apollo and the muses.

"Thoreau, in 1851, records this flower in bloom November 7th": Thoreau's complete *Journal* (14 vols.) was not published until 1906, in an edition edited by Bradford Torrey and Francis H. Allen. Wright may have learned of the entry from Torrey, because it does not appear in an earlier version of the journal published as *Autumn: From the Journal of Henry D. Thoreau* (New York: Houghton, Mifflin, 1892), edited by H. G. O. Blake. William Ellery Channing's *Thoreau: The Poet-Naturalist* (Boston: Roberts Brothers, 1873) notes Thoreau's encounter with a gentian on November 7, but does not record the year (93).

"Bryant found it even later, among the Cummington hills": Bryant, "November" (1824). Bryant was born in Cummington, Massachusetts.

"they bloom at Michaelmas, when the farmer eats his goose": Michaelmas Day, 29 September, is the festival of St. Michael and all Angels. The custom of eating goose at Michaelmas may derive from geese being plentiful and in good condition at this season.

120 "Now comes . . . the Northern Spy": Difficult reading because of its combination of botanical and bibliographical references, this paragraph probably reflects the influence of Wright's husband, a rare book dealer. Wright refers to: Izaak Walton (1593–1683), best known for *The Compleat Angler*, first published in 1653 and largely rewritten for the second edition, published in 1655; levant, a type of heavy, coarse-grained morocco leather used in bookbinding; Cornelius Jansen (1585–1638), a Dutch theologian whose arguments in favor of predestination came to be known as "Jansenism" (although Jansenism closely resembled Calvinism, Jansenists were fiercely vocal Roman Catholics, and, as the movement was elaborated in France, they also came to embrace an austere piety and rigorous morality—hence the "untempered" style of the fervid red leather); and "Laus Veneris" (1866), one of Swinburne's most notorious, sexually explicit poems, which is a retelling of the Tannhäuser legend "In Praise of Venus." Wright also mentions the *Herball or Generall Historie of Plantes* (1597) of John Gerard (1545–1612); Jean Grolier de Serviéres (1479–1565), a French bibliophile; and T. J. Cobden-Sanderson (1840–1922), a British bookbinder.

121 "Veuve Cliquot": Champagne produced by Veuve Clicquot-Ponsardin, a large and influential house, founded in 1772.

"John o' Dreams": A stupid, dreamy fellow, absent of mind and half asleep.

122 "leashed by ivy and 'lush woodbine' ": The appearance of this phrase in the poem "Wedded Love" (l. 107) by Gerald Massey (1828–1907) may account for Wright's quotation of it here.

A WINTER MOOD

127 "Here might I pause and bend in reverence": William Wordsworth (1770–1850), *The Prelude* (1850), XIII.224–25.

132 "one more tint to the palet": Palette.

134 "Two lighthouses stand at the reef-points": Penfield Reef Light, built in 1874, lies one mile south of the Fairfield shoreline and marks the end of a long, curving reef exposed above water at low tide. Black Rock Harbor Light, built in 1809 and rebuilt in 1923, is located on the south end of Fayerweather Island southeast of Fairfield.

"the bells of St. Mary's hang silent": "St. Mary's By-the-Sea," built in 1893 and demolished in 1925, was a small, picturesque church in Bridgeport, noted for its specially made chimes.

"the sun . . . has now reached its solstitial turning": 21 or 22 December, when the sun reaches its extreme southern point in the ecliptic; midwinter.

135 "Our Dr. Holmes . . . wrote in a letter thus": Unpublished letter in author's possession [Wright's note]. Oliver Wendell Holmes (1809–94), American physician and author. The letter, dated 21 August 1879, Beverly Farms, Massachusetts, is part of Wright's Autograph Album (FPL). Wright's transcription contains a few minor errors. Holmes's references include the following: Pisgah is the mountain from which Moses was allowed to view the Promised Land; the River Jordan, west of Mount Pisgah, separated the wilderness of the world from the Promised Land and is a symbol of the crossing over into death; "The days of our years are threescore years and ten; / and if by reason of strength they be fourscore years, / yet is their strength labour and sorrow; / for it is soon cut off, and we fly away" (Psalms 90.10); William Ewart Gladstone (1809–98), British prime minister (four times between 1868 and 1894); Benjamin Disraeli (1804–81), British prime minister (1868 and 1874–80), author, and diplomat; Johann Joseph Wenzel Radetzky von Radetz (1766–1858), who served as governor-general of Lombardy-Venetia through his ninety-first year; Thomas Parr (1483?–1635), "Old Parr," who was reputed to have lived 152 years; Henry Jenkins (d. 1670), who was reputed to have lived 169 years; the Lord said to Joshua: "From the wilderness and this Lebanon even unto the great river, the river Euphrates, all the land of the Hittites, and unto the great sea toward the going down of the sun, shall be your coast" (Joshua 1.4).

Selected Bibliography

MAJOR WORKS BY MABEL OSGOOD WRIGHT

Published by the Macmillan Company, New York

The Friendship of Nature: A New England Chronicle of Birds and Flowers (1894).
Birdcraft: A Field Book of Two Hundred Song, Game, and Water Birds (1895).
Tommy-Anne and the Three Hearts (1896).
Citizen Bird: Scenes from Bird-life in Plain English for Beginners (1897), with Elliott Coues.
Four-Footed Americans and Their Kin (1898), ed. Frank Chapman.
Wabeno, the Magician: The Sequel to "Tommy-Anne and the Three Hearts" (1899).
The Dream Fox Story Book (1900).
Flowers and Ferns in Their Haunts (1901).
The Garden of a Commuter's Wife (1901).
Dogtown: Being Some Chapters from the Annals of the Waddles Family, Set Down in the Language of Housepeople (1902).
Aunt Jimmy's Will (1903).
People of the Whirlpool: From the Experience Book of a Commuter's Wife (1903).
Stories of Earth and Sky (1904).
Second Reader: Stories of Plants and Animals (1904).
Third Reader: Stories of Birds and Beasts (1904).
The Woman Errant: Being Some Chapters from the Wonder Book of Barbara, the Commuter's Wife (1904).
At the Sign of the Fox: A Romance (1905).
The Garden, You, and I (1906).
The Heart of Nature (1906).
Gray Lady and the Birds: Stories of the Bird Year for Home and School (1907).
The Open Window: Tales of the Months (1908).
Poppea of the Post Office (1909).
Princess Flower Hat: A Comedy from the Perplexity Book of Barbara, the Commuter's Wife (1910).
The Love That Lives (1911).
The Stranger at the Gate: A Story of Christmas (1913).
My New York (1926).
Captains of the Watch of Life and Death (1927).
Eudora's Men (1931).

SECONDARY SOURCES

Barrow, Mark V. *A Passion for Birds: American Ornithology after Audubon.* Princeton: Princeton Univ. Press, 1998.

Battalio, John T. *The Rhetoric of Science in the Evolution of American Ornithological Discourse.* Stamford, Conn.: Ablex, 1998.

Brooks, Paul. *Speaking for Nature: How Literary Naturalists from Henry Thoreau to Rachel Carson Have Shaped America.* Boston: Houghton Mifflin, 1980.

Doughty, Robin W. *Feather Fashions and Bird Preservation: A Study in Nature Protection.* Berkeley: Univ. of California Press, 1975.

Dunlap, Thomas R. *Saving America's Wildlife.* Princeton: Princeton Univ. Press, 1988.

Fox, Stephen R. *John Muir and His Legacy: The American Conservation Movement.* Boston: Little, Brown, 1981.

Gibbons, Felton, and Deborah Strom. *Neighbors to the Birds: A History of Birdwatching in America.* New York: Norton, 1988.

Graham, Frank. *The Audubon Ark: A History of the National Audubon Society.* New York: Knopf, 1990.

Kastner, Joseph. *A World of Watchers.* New York: Knopf, 1986.

Lutts, Ralph. *The Nature Fakers: Wildlife, Science, and Sentiment.* Golden, Colo.: Fulcrum, 1990.

Lyon, Thomas J. *This Incomperable Lande: A Book of American Nature Writing.* Boston: Houghton Mifflin, 1989.

Mighetto, Lisa. *Wild Animals and American Environmental Ethics.* Tucson: Univ. of Arizona Press, 1991.

Norwood, Vera. *Made from This Earth: American Women and Nature.* Chapel Hill: Univ. of North Carolina Press, 1993.

Orr, Oliver H. Jr. *Saving American Birds: T. Gilbert Pearson and the Founding of the Audubon Movement.* Gainesville: Univ. Press of Florida, 1992.

Schmitt, Peter J. *Back to Nature: The Arcadian Myth in Urban America.* 1969. Baltimore: Johns Hopkins Univ. Press, 1990.

Welker, Robert Henry. *Birds and Men: American Birds in Science, Art, Literature, and Conservation, 1800–1900.* Cambridge: Harvard Univ. Press, 1955.

Index of Common and Scientific Names

This index follows Wright's text in its terminology, hyphenation, and italicization. Although several names refer to the same species, page numbers apply only to the appearance of the listed name.

Other Books in the Series

The Desert: Further Studies in Natural Appearances
John C. Van Dyke
with a critical introduction by Peter Wild

This Hill, This Valley
Hal Borland
with drawings by Peter Marks

On the Shore of the Sundown Sea
T. H. Watkins
with illustrations by Earl Thollander

Siftings
Jens Jensen
foreword by Charles E. Little
afterword by Darrel G. Morrison

Library of Congress Cataloging-in-Publication Data

Wright, Mabel Osgood, 1859–1934.
The friendship of nature : a New England chronicle of birds and
flowers / by Mabel Osgood Wright ; with photographs by the author ;
edited by Daniel J. Philippon.
     p.   cm. – (American land classics)
Originally published: New York : Macmillan, 1894.
Includes bibliographical references.
ISBN 0-8018-6234-5 (alk. paper). –
ISBN 0-8018-6223-X pbk. : alk. paper)
  1. Natural history–Outdoor books.   I. Philippon, Daniel J.
II. Title.   III. Series.
QH81.W794   1999
508.74–dc21   99-20198